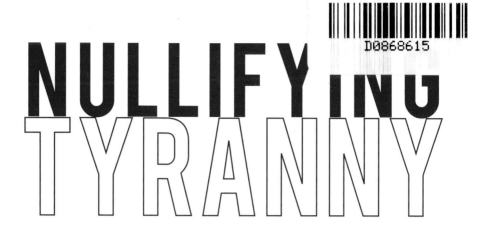

NULLIFYING TYRANNY

Creating Moral Communities in an Immoral Society

James Ronald Kennedy
and Walter Donald Kennedy

PELICAN PUBLISHING COMPANY
GRETNA 2010

*The word "Pelican" and the depiction of a pelican
are trademarks of Pelican Publishing Company, Inc.,
and are registered in the U.S. Patent and Trademark Office.*

Library of Congress Cataloging-in-Publication Data

Kennedy, James Ronald.
  Nullifying tyranny : creating moral communities in an immoral
society / by James Ronald Kennedy and Walter Donald Kennedy.
    p. cm.
  Includes bibliographical references and index.
  ISBN 978-1-58980-779-2 (pbk. : alk. paper) 1. Nullification (States'
rights) 2. Federal government—United States. 3. United States—
Moral conditions. I. Kennedy, Walter Donald. II. Title.
  JK311.K46 2010
  261.7—dc22
                              2009052007

All Scripture quotations are from *The New Scofield Reference Bible*
(KJV): New York-Oxford University Press © 1967 by Oxford
University Press. All rights reserved. Used by permission.

Printed in the United States of America
Published by Pelican Publishing Company, Inc.
1000 Burmaster Street, Gretna, Louisiana 70053

The authors are well aware of the debt of love and honor we owe to those who came before us and left for our benefit a legacy of Christian faithfulness to family and community. Added to that legacy is our personal memory of faithful Christian parents who, while poor by earthly standards, were rich in the things of God. Our memories begin in the small community of Pearl Valley in rural Mississippi. Our mother and father lived the life they faithfully professed as Sunday School teacher and deacon of Pearl Valley Baptist Church.

In the hope that this book will in some small way encourage others to be equally faithful to their calling to be the Lord's witness in this sinful world:

We dedicate this book to the memory of our mother, Lennie Mae Kennedy (1917-2006), and our father, Burnice E. Kennedy (1909-1988).

Contents

Introduction

"Jesus is humiliated in new ways even today when things that are most holy and profound in the faith are being trivialized, the sense of the sacred is allowed to erode. Values and norms that held societies together and drew people to higher ideals are laughed at and thrown overboard. Jesus continues to be ridiculed."

Pope Benedict XVI,
2009 Good Friday address[1]

"We are going to discover that cultural Christianity is what eventually disappears in a secularized age...it's going to be a very different situation for the pastor of the First Baptist Church to worry about being arrested...we are not as many as we thought..."

Albert Mohler Jr.,
President Southern Baptist Theological Seminary[2]

Who Should Read This Book?

This book is written for a special group of people. It is written for fellow Christians who at some level understand that the government of these United States has been slowly taken over and for some time has been under the control of or dominated by an anti-Christian secular humanist element that constitutes an aggressive political faction. We are writing to Christians who hold firm to the faith of our fathers regardless of how hopeless the struggle may appear to man. It is the authors' desire to demonstrate to God's people that hope is not lost—"we the people" who hold Christian moral values still have the potential to rise up, throw off the bondage of a secular

---

1. http://www.dailymail.co.uk/news/worldnews/article-1169030/Pope-warns-desert-godlessness-Good-Friday-address.html (accessed April 12, 2009).
2. www.lafamilyforum.org/node/104 (accessed May 17, 2009)

9

humanist society, and establish moral communities in which our values can be safely passed on to the next generation of Christians. We wish to demonstrate that moral communities begin with moral individuals and extend to the nuclear family, the extended family, and the community. The creation of moral communities depends on the ability of "we the people" to control vital social issues at the level of our individual home state which was once known as a sovereign state. This control can become a reality only by dramatic but plausible political action—action taken not to gain political power, but to destroy the system of power, perks, and privileges used by America's ruling elite to foist a secular humanist agenda upon God's people.

An Explanation of Ideas

The central theme of this book is that the political system devised by the founding fathers and handed down to "we the people" has been perverted and distorted by special interest groups. These special interest groups now use the power of the Federal government to advance their social agenda while at the same time enacting laws that repress traditional Christian morality and are destructive of traditional family values. Perhaps some God-fearing, law-abiding, taxpaying Americans may object to the notion that the United States today is an immoral nation with a secular humanist ruling elite that dominates America's moral values. The authors hope that a careful and prayerful reading of these simple pages will convince these God-fearing people to change their opinion and join with us to remake this country into the type of nation that our Christian founding fathers bequeathed to us. We believe that America's current political system is broken, and, if Christian moral values are to survive in the United States, there must be a radical restoration of America's political institutions—back to the form and functions intended by the founding fathers when they gave "we the people" a constitutionally limited republic of republics.

Biblical Governance

Many Christians think that God is silent when it comes to the type of government He prefers for His people. We will give the reader specific examples from the Scriptures of God's preference for and establishment of limited government for His people. God also warned His people about the dangers of big government—although the Scriptures do not use the exact words, the warning to avoid all-powerful centralized government is very clear and undeniable! We will also demonstrate from the Scriptures that God proclaims that His people must respect their neighbors' private property rights. All of these scriptural examples are relevant for us today as we make plans for the inauguration of a system of government that supports the establishment of moral communities.

Key Terms

The forgotten man: "We the people" who do not have political power at the Federal level have become America's forgotten men and women. We are the ones who pay the taxes that are used to finance a government whose agenda all too often centers on programs and policies that are detrimental to Christian values. The ruling elite occasionally, especially during an election, give lip service to our social and moral concerns, but they never enact laws that support our interests, or better yet repeal laws detrimental to our interests. The forgotten man is part of America's productive element that creates wealth and improves living standards generation to generation.

The ruling elite: Those who hold political power on the Federal level and those close to or allied with those who hold Federal political power are now the ruling elite in America. This group includes both Democratic and Republican elected officials. The primary purpose of the ruling elite is to maintain the *status quo* because it provides them the perks, privileges, and power that they enjoy. The ruling elite is composed of liberals, nominal socialists, secular humanists, and Washington conservatives, all of whom have a vested interest in maintaining America's current political system. Those close to the ruling elite are their supporters who provide the funding for the multimillion-dollar political campaigns for public office and special interest groups that depend on the ruling elite to funnel large amounts of taxpayers' money to their special interest group or cause. The ruling elite, their supporters, and politically correct allies represent the parasitic elements in America's contemporary political system.

Other people's money (OPM): This is tax money that is collected by force or by implied threat of force from the forgotten man and redistributed to the clients, friends, and political allies of the ruling elite. This money collected from Christians is used to fund abortion on demand, so-called homosexual rights activity, quasi-pornographic sex education in public schools, and a host of other immoral activities. OPM extracted from the productive element of American society represents 40 to 60 percent of the working man's income. It is, and has been for more than fifty years, the primary means that nominal socialists use to redistribute wealth from the productive members of society to the parasitic members of society.

Nominal socialists: This term is used to describe those who believe that government has the right to extort money from those who honestly produce it (OPM) and redistribute it to those whom they have determined deserve it. In Great Britain they would be known as Fabian socialists. They are distinctly different from Marxist socialists, but the net effect is little different. As a group, liberals, secular humanists, and unfortunately most Washington "conservatives" are to one degree or another nominal socialists.

How This Book Is Organized

Section I   **Godly Separation from Evil,** chapters 1 through 3: A discussion of God's requirement for His people to be separate from evil, God's warnings about the dangers posed by powerful government, His requirement for His people to be productive members of society while respecting the property rights of their fellows.

Section II   **Godly Principles of Limited Government,** chapters 4 through 13: Ten basic principles necessary for the establishment of legitimate, limited, and moral government that serves as the political support and defender of a moral community.

Section III   **Godly Republic Lost—Godly Republic Regained,** chapters 14 through 20: A discussion of America's Christian moral foundations and the founding fathers' original intentions to establish a limited republic of republics, explains how the founding fathers' original intentions were distorted and perverted by special interests seeking to gain material advantage by controlling the Federal government, explains how "we the people" can reclaim our lost estate of liberty and establish moral communities within those states that have moral majorities.

Addendum: 1. **Katrina: Death by Government:** An article by Ron Kennedy outlining how government set in motion the events that led to the unnecessary human tragedy occurring during Hurricane Katrina.

2. **Dixie's Unwelcomed Presence in Rosie O'Donnell's America:** An article by Ron Kennedy contrasting the Bible Belt's moral and social values with the secular humanist values held by America's ruling elite.

3. **Consent of the Governed—Key to Liberty:** An article by Donnie Kennedy demonstrating the rich heritage of intellectual thought on which the American principle of consent of the governed is built and its relation to the American right of secession.

4. **Boom-Bust Economics—A Joy for the Ruling Elite But a Disaster for the Forgotten Man:** An article by Ron Kennedy explaining how America's ruling elite cause economic booms and busts that result in economic bubbles such as the housing bubble. The ruling elite use all such crises to enrich themselves and their supporters and to enlarge their political power— all such gains for the ruling elite are eventually paid for by the forgotten man.

NULLIFYING
TYRANNY

.

Section I

Godly Separation from Evil

1

Be Ye Separate—
God's Command for Moral People

"Wherefore, come out from among them, and be ye separate, saith the Lord, and touch not the unclean thing; and I will receive you."

2 Corinthians 6:17

Can good safely dwell with evil? In human society will good pull evil up, or will evil pull good down? What communion does light have with darkness (2 Corinthians 6:14)? Most Christians recognize the importance of these questions in regard to spiritual life, but they are equally important socially and politically. Indeed, the answer to these questions may well determine whether or not America's Christian moral traditions will be passed on to another generation.

A Moral People in an Immoral Nation

Can moral people survive in an immoral nation? Can they pass their standards on to their children while living in an immoral society? What would have happened to Lot's family had he elected to ignore God's warning to depart from the wickedness of Gomorrah? Are Americans living in the moral equivalent of Gomorrah? We recently had a discussion with a young father who was very concerned about the effect society was having on his two young daughters. He and his wife were trying to raise their children in a Christian home environment, they were active in their church, they were paying to send their children to schools operated by their church, they set and lived by moral standards; yet the values they were trying to pass on to their children were radically different from the values the secular world was advocating. He noted that the previous night their daughters were watching a program on television that had always been acceptable, but this time it was about a teenager who was pregnant and was planning to give her baby up for adoption—to a "gay" couple. He then asked, "How can we compete with an immoral world—what chance do we have

19

against such overwhelming evil?" An age-old question—how do the righteous survive in a society ruled by the unrighteous?

God's Word is very plain—it tells us to be separate—but it does not tell moral Americans *how* to be separate. Some things are left for us to work out, and with God's help we can devise a way to separate the moral from the immoral and lead lives that stand as living testimonies to the goodness and mercy of our loving God. The principle of separation recommended in 2 Corinthians 6:17 is not a command for God's people to cloister themselves away in communes. As God's people we have a duty to serve as a living example to those around us and by our example help to draw the lost to the Lord. We have a duty to develop moral communities that will support the efforts of families to raise their children in a manner that is pleasing to God. But, how can moral communities be developed in a nation that has spent the past fifty years or more consumed with hedonistic pleasure-seeking, especially while the nation is increasingly "slouching toward Gomorrah"?[1]

There is an underlying principle in God's call to be separate—God will not bless a people who by their choice embrace evil or through their apathy enable evil. It is not by chance that we are admonished in Proverbs that "righteousness exalteth a nation, but sin is a reproach to any people."[2] This presents a difficult problem for contemporary America. Will God continue to bless this nation when its government advocates policies and programs that promote anti-Christian secular humanist ideology? What happens to a once righteous nation when those who do not believe in moral standards based on biblical principles outvote those who do?

In the American democracy as it is currently structured, majority rule is just that—if those advocating recognition of marriage between homosexuals can gain a simple majority in a national vote, then their candidates can foist their will upon the minority who find such an agenda an abomination. In later chapters we will see that this is not the type of government America's founding fathers intended—

1. This phrase comes from the title of former Supreme Court nominee Robert Bork's book *Slouching Towards Gomorrah: Modern Liberalism and American Decline* (New York: Regan Books, 1996).
2. Proverbs 14:34.

government has been perverted to serve the interests of those who have little in common with America's founding principles. But this can be corrected—thus allowing moral people to obey God's command, "Be ye separate!"

Believers Yoked Together with Unbelievers

Three verses prior to the one quoted in 2 Corinthians 6:17 God warns His people not to be "yoked together with unbelievers" (v. 14). The image of a yoke was very real to the people in Corinth. Every day they would see draft animals yoked together pulling a load in a cart or plowing a field. The image of two working together to accomplish a common goal is very important. Believers are admonished not to allow themselves to be yoked together with unbelievers for the purpose of accomplishing an immoral task. How does this scripture apply to moral people in America today? Because we live in a mass democracy that follows the principle of majority rule, if immoral people gain control of government they can use the force of government to compel the minority who disagree with them to obey the rules established by those who, by majority rule, control government. Government can take money via taxation away from moral people and use that money to pay lawyers to file suits against schools that allow Christian groups to meet on their premises. This is but one example of thousands of others that occur every day in this country. Whether we like it or not, our money is used by government to finance numerous activities that we would consider immoral—yet, in America's current political system, we are yoked together with the majority. God commands us, "Be ye not unequally yoked together with unbelievers"[3]; but the national government commands us to supply our share of the funds necessary for the government to wage war against our Christian values. It has become such a common occurrence that most of us have learned to ignore it—not because we agree, but because up to now no one has offered a way to stop such activities by "our" government.

Separate from Whom or What?

When people hear the command to separate it is usually taken

---

3. 2 Corinthians 6:14.

as a command to separate from ungodly people. But as already noted we do not advocate removing ourselves from society and living a cloistered life. In this book we advocate reclaiming our original American right to control what happens in our extended communities. As our country was originally established it was possible to be politically separate without requiring physical separation as was practiced by many universalists and utopian dreamers in the early nineteenth century.[4] Moral people should not seek to be physically separated from the rest of the world. Moral people have a duty to be living witnesses, to be a light in a dark world, to be living evidence that there is One Who can redeem fallen man. Every Christian's prayer should be, "Dear Jesus, help me to spread Your fragrance everywhere I go so that every soul I come in contact with may feel Your presence in my soul."[5] Our duty to be living witnesses for Jesus cannot be done if we are physically separated from the lost. Christians also have a duty to make sure that government does not use its supra-personal power to fight against our moral values. To accomplish this requires political not physical separation. It is not people that we must separate ourselves from, but a political system that abuses its constitutional powers to the detriment of moral, law-abiding, taxpaying citizens.

The moral imperative for moral people to politically separate ourselves from the current political system is especially evident when we consider the command to avoid being yoked together with unbelievers. God's people should not allow their resources to be used to promote ungodly ideology. Yet in the current political system there is nothing the average person can do to halt or even avoid this practice. That is why this book is necessary—we *can* do something, and if we can, in fact, do something, then it becomes our moral duty to do it!

Many who first read these lines may take exception to the fact that America is described in such a low term—as a sinful nation. Indeed the Jeremiahs of the world are never popular—especially with the

---

4. For example, socialist communes seeking to perfect man by organizing and taking action to correct the evils in human society as established by The Oneida Community, The Fourierist, and The Shakers.

5. From Mother Teresa's prayer, "Radiating Christ," as cited in *Jesus Is My All in All*, edited by Brian Kolodiejchuk, M.C. (New York: Doubleday, 2008), p. 48.

ruling elite.[6] Also, many moral, law-abiding, taxpaying citizens have confused the concept of patriotism with the idea that we must accept everything that the America government does without question or else we are unpatriotic. Loving our country does not mean that we must accept everything immoral elected officials have done to our country. Being loyal to one's country does not require an individual to accept as unchangeable the immoral condition to which his country has fallen. Being patriotic does not mean moral Americans must blindly accept the dictates of a government controlled by those who openly express hatred for our moral views. Being "100 percent" American does not mean we must compromise our moral beliefs. It does not mean we must refuse to insist that government be based on a morally acceptable political philosophy. With that said—let us go to the next chapter titled "America the Sinful."

6. The term "ruling elite" is used in this book to describe those who hold the power of government. In a mass democracy such as we now have in America that would be those who hold elected office. In addition it includes those who have close ties, usually financial ties, to those in elected office and the bureaucracy that administers the day-to-day activities of government. "Elite" specifically refers to the fact that most elected officials have a virtual guarantee on their office once elected— the high incumbency rate is not due to the great job they do protecting the rights and property of "we the people," but to the fact that they can use the perks, privileges, and power of their public office to assure their re-election.

2

America the Sinful

"Sin is a reproach to any people."

Proverbs 14:34

It is easy for those of us who were children in the mid to late 1950s to understand how low American morals have sunk. We have a point of reference that allows us to compare what we have today to what we had back then. In medicine an insidious disease is one that sickens and eventually kills the patient but does so very slowly over a long period of time—a period of time so long the patient never realizes how sick he actually is until it is too late to apply the healing treatment. Today it is common to travel public highways and see large billboards advertising triple X-rated video stores. Such public advertisement of immorality would never have been allowed in the "Bible Belt" in the late 1950s and highly unlikely even in what we now refer to as the "Blue" states. The vulgarity and coarseness of bumper stickers and tee shirts did not occur overnight but gradually "slipped" up on us until today moral people don't even take note of such "benign" vulgarity. Yet, the constant "dumbing down" of what is morally acceptable in society has an insidiously evil impact on the family, our children, and our society.

The following data should be helpful for those who do not have a clear "frame of reference" to judge the decay of American moral values. In 1940 a survey was taken asking teachers to identify the five most serious problems facing teachers and students in America's schools. They identified the following: (1) talking out of turn, (2) chewing gum, (3) making noise, (4) running in halls, and (5) cutting in line. Half a century later the survey was repeated, and teachers in 1990 identified the following problems: (1) drug abuse, (2) alcohol abuse, (3) pregnancy, (4) suicide, and (5) rape. America's decline into immorality did not happen overnight. It happened gradually— so gradually that most Americans did not even notice the immoral forces working to pervert America's moral fiber.

Immorality has increased exponentially in America since the early 1960s. If silence gives consent, then American Christians have, by our inaction, given consent to the demonization of traditional Christian moral values. In the fifty years since 1960 the rate of single parenthood increased more than 300 percent. In contemporary America more than 25 percent, one in four, children are born into single-parent homes. Anyone who has studied the economic impact of single parenthood understands the negative impact it has on the child and society. The likelihood of childhood poverty, with all the social pathologies that go with poverty, greatly (exponentially) increases for a child raised outside of a stable traditional family.

Crime is another area that has increased dramatically in America[1] over time. In the 1920s when four gangsters, in faraway Chicago, killed seven other gangsters on St. Valentines' Day, the country was shocked and horrified. It made headlines across the country and merited a couple of entries in the *World Book Encyclopedia*. Gang killings are so common today that they hardly make back-page coverage. It is as if Americans have learned to ignore the gunshots, step over the bodies, and go on with their lives.

Volumes of data could be cited,[2] but data alone will not explain how our society became so corrupt and perverted. Things that were abominable to one generation have become commonplace and acceptable for the next generation! And even worse, these downward trends show no sign of slowing, much less reversing. What happened? How long will God's people remain complacent while evil overtakes our society? Or is it complacency—perhaps we have learned to be indifferent to things we cannot control. If that is the case, then the question is, "How long will God's people wait before taking bold—even audacious—action to change the perverted system that has foisted such immorality upon our society?"

Some have offered an explanation, though it is only a part of the whole explanation of how we as a society slowly became complacent with social conditions that would have repulsed our mothers and fathers. Their explanation is that society can tolerate only so much

    1. See James Ronald Kennedy and Walter Donald Kennedy, *Why Not Freedom!* (Gretna, LA: Pelican Publishing Company, 1994), p. 95.
    2. Ibid., pp. 63-240.

perversion or deviancy for social norms.[3] If something happens that causes an increase in deviancy (for example; government changes its approach to crime from prevention and punishment to rehabilitating offenders, and as a result there is a dramatic increase in crime) society will adjust to the new level by redefining deviancy downward. Now, by the magic of redefining deviancy—deviancy as measured by the new politically correct lower standard—the new amount of deviancy is back down to an acceptable level! In this way, prior deviant behavior is socially redeemed and pronounced normal behavior. It is almost like the old joke, "Why not legalize everything, and then there will be no crime!"

It is important to note that defining deviancy downward cannot occur in a moral society in the absence of a compelling and oppressive force, or threat of force. The compelling force comes from outside the moral community—the people are led astray by evil leaders, and the moral remnant is forced into hiding. In the past, morally corrupting force has come from corrupted religious leaders[4] or from government. Once the effort to define deviancy downward begins, it is only a short time before those *promoting* deviancy begin the effort to define deviancy upward. Not only is the effort made to normalize behavior that was *formerly considered deviant,* but those who control the social force of society soon begin the effort to redefine formerly normal values to turn them into deviant behavior or values. In modern times it is always government that controls the social forces that are used to change and remake society. Politically correct speech codes are an example of how government is used to foist immoral social change on society by defining formerly normal—moral—behavior as immoral behavior.

Government-financed and government-controlled education

---

3. Daniel Patrick Moynihan, interview on PBS at www.pbs.org/fmc/interviews/moynihan.htm (accessed 4/12/2009).

4. Recall that Jesus denounced the religious leaders of His day and called them "whited sepulchres" in Matthew 23:27. Jeremiah demonstrated how much evil can be done when evil religious leaders combine with evil governmental leaders when he brought God's message to Judah, "The priests said not, Where is the Lord? And they that handle the law knew me not. The rulers also transgressed against me, and the prophets prophesied by Baal, and walked after things that do not profit" (Jeremiah 2:8).

institutions have been turned into propaganda institutes to promote secular humanist, nominal socialist, and liberal ideas. It makes no difference to government that such ideas are diametrically opposite of the values of the taxpayers whose money is used to finance the liberal propaganda efforts. "We the people" are actually paying to have our children brainwashed by secular humanists.

At the University of Michigan a student of religion offered the opinion that homosexuality is immoral according to the teachings of the Bible. He was singled out by university leaders for punishment and ordered to attend sensitivity training and obtain other reeducation. The government-controlled university did not care about academic freedom, freedom of speech, or the fact that the student was advocating a belief held by a large segment of the taxpayers who were being forced by the government tax collector to pay for the university. Not only was the student's liberty violated, but, and this was the most important thing as far as the politically correct university was concerned, the public humiliation and harassment of the outspoken, religious student served to cool free speech. It served to de-motivate other students from making politically incorrect statements. It served notice on all students that biblical values were no longer "normal," but in the politically correct, secular humanist world, such outdated values had become abnormal and deviant. Anyone expressing such abnormal and deviant behavior would be publicly humiliated and punished! Every freedom-loving, God-fearing American should ask, "What is happening to freedom of religion and freedom of speech in America, and how can we resist these evil efforts?"

At the University of Pennsylvania a group of African-American female students were creating a loud and offensive noise outside dorm rooms where other students were trying to sleep or study. A white student called the rowdy students "behemahs" and demanded they leave. No one at the university knew what "behemahs" meant (perhaps the student meant "behemoths" meaning large animals), but because the noisemakers were black, and the individual making the remark was white, the university decided it was a racial attack! The student faced the public humiliation of being charged with "hate speech" and being held up as a public example of a cruel racist. The university attempted to force him to confess and admit his guilt—even though no one could find any evidence that his statement was racially motivated. The message was clear: "In our society any person who dares to speak in a politically incorrect manner, even unintentionally, will receive the full wrath of those who control our society." And remember: (1) the university's politically correct warning was intended not just for the offender but for everyone, and (2) these politically correct efforts were paid for by moral, law-abiding taxpayers, many if not most of whom would not have approved of such acts by those in authority.

The secular humanists, liberals, and nominal socialists who now control our society do not care about the degrading effect that their policies are having on society. Their primary goal is to remake society by destroying the last vestige of the old, antiquated, Bible-based society and replace it with a system in which they are freely allowed to use the force of government to foist their worldview upon the moral remnant who refuse to voluntarily renounce "old" ways and accept the new secular humanist order.

Evidence as to how the change from a Bible-based society (a society that believes in absolute, unchangeable values based on God's Word) to the new secular humanist society is most evident in America's inner cities.[5] Inner cities are populated primarily by African-Americans who have been targeted to receive a major portion of government programs and projects—all at the behest of liberal, nominal socialist politicians and social activists who control or influence government policy. What has been the effect on the people who live in the inner cities after almost half a century of these government programs? African-American conservative educator and columnist Walter Williams noted:

> Black illegitimacy stands at 70 percent; nearly 50 percent of black students drop out of high school; and only 30 percent of black youngsters reside in two-parent families. In 2005, while 13 percent of the population, blacks committed over 52 percent of the nation's homicides...[6]

5. America's slide into immorality is most evident in the inner cites, but social immorality is by no means the exclusive vice of the inner cities; it affects all areas of the nation.

6. Walter E. Williams, "A Nation of Cowards," February 25, 2009, www.townhall.com (accessed 2/26/2009).

The truly astonishing and sad fact is that there were more stable black families during the era of slavery and governmentally enforced Jim Crow segregation laws than there are now under the rule of liberals and nominal socialists! An important rule to remember is that the policies promoted by nominal socialists always end up hurting the people they claim to be helping. In the middle of the Jim Crow segregation era, the 1940s, black illegitimacy was 19 percent, in 1950 (still the era of Jim Crow segregation) it was 18 percent, but today it is 70 percent! "Both during slavery and as late as 1920, a teenage girl raising a child without a man present was rare among blacks."[7] Not really a good record for the social policies of liberals, nominal socialist politicians, and social activists. Yet, failure is not important to liberals and nominal socialists—what is important is that they are using taxpayers' money to reshape society to fit their vision of a socially "just" America.

William Booth, founder of the Salvation Army, is reported to have said, "You can't get the man out of the gutter unless first you get the gutter out of the man." This is why human effort to improve the human condition by concentrating on redistributing material goods from those who have to those who do not have will always fail. Only God is capable of getting the gutter out of man. Liberals, secular humanists, and nominal socialists try to blame the failure of their policies in the inner cities on the remaining effects of slavery and racism. As bad as slavery was or racial hatred is—moral people should not be afraid to point out that the problem facing an immoral nation is fundamentally deeper than the legacy of prior slavery, racial hatred, or an unjust distribution of wealth. Government is not equipped to deal with this fundamental human need. Star Parker, who by her own effort pulled herself out of inner-city poverty, noted the inability of government to deal with this human need:

> A centralized, secular government may insist that in order to help this broken woman it needs to build more tax-funded clinics in her neighborhood, but how would this address the source of her poverty? Shame and despair have enslaved her to self-destruction. Her poverty is internal and political socialism cannot adequately address conditions of the heart. That is the work of religion.[8]

7. Ibid.
8. Star Parker, *Uncle Sam's Plantation* (Nashville, TN: WND Books, 2003), p. 30.

America's inner cites are extreme examples of the failure of liberal, nominal socialist social engineering programs. Because the population of inner cities is predominately black, many think such problems are a result of the people (blacks) when in reality the problem is with the social programs foisted upon the people living in inner cites. The results would be the same if the population was predominantly white—the evil originates from the fallen condition of man and is made worse by liberal governmental social programs that discourage self-reliance and individual responsibility.

Similar failures occur in nations that adopt liberal, nominal socialist social programs for recipients who are predominantly white. Dr. Theodore Dalrymple is an English physician who worked with the white underclass in England. He noted the failure of liberal social welfare in modern Britain:

> Not that government is blameless in the matter—far from it. Intellectuals propounded the idea that man should be freed from the shackles of social convention and self-control, and the government, without any demand from below, enacted laws that promoted unrestrained behavior and created a welfare system that protected people from some of its economic consequences. When the barriers to evil are brought down, it flourishes; and never again will I be tempted to believe in the fundamental goodness of man, or that evil is something exceptional or alien to human nature.[9]

The human heart, spiritually speaking, is the same regardless of skin color. Humans are all in need of moral redemption—god-government, like all false gods, cannot cure man's most basic human deficiency. Social degeneracy is the ultimate result when government pushes aside basic moral principles and attempts to socially engineer society according to a secular humanist vision of a "fair and just" world. Good intentions do not guarantee good outcomes, nor do they excuse the human tragedy that lies in the wake of such human efforts to perfect man.

America's fall into degeneracy and perversion, its acceptance of gross immorality as "normal," did not occur overnight. It

9. Theodore Dalrymple, *Our Culture, What's Left of It* (Chicago: Ivan R. Dee, 2005), p. 9.

occurred gradually, and it was encouraged by political leaders who saw in liberalism and nominal socialism a means to assure their incumbency. America's trip down the road to Gomorrah would not have occurred had it not been for the corrupting influence of big government. If government is such a threat to human liberty and morality, then surely God would have warned His people about the dangers posed by human government. The sad but overlooked fact is that God did indeed warn His people, but His people are all too often prone to forget!

3

The Inherent Evil of Government—God's Warning

"And the Lord said…they have rejected me, that I should not reign over them."
1 Samuel 8:7

Perfection is in all of God's creation. He created a perfect world, then created a perfect man and woman, and placed them in a prefect garden. Man's responsibility was to glorify his Creator and follow His simple rule not to eat of the fruit of the tree of knowledge of good and evil—"For in the day that thou eatest thereof thou shalt surely die" (Genesis 2:17). In the garden man did not need human government, but once sin entered into the human story, then government became necessary. At first it was government of patriarchs, an extended family with one man serving as judge for disputes and enforcer of social rules of conduct. Father Abraham serves as an example of such human government. But as man's numbers increased, governmental power was assumed by men whose motive was no longer to serve the needs of the extended family but to serve themselves and those close to them—even though this required the rulers to oppress their subjects.

The people of Israel had a long history in which they had experienced good (limited) government by Father Abraham. Under this government the people were in essence a local community. This type of government encouraged self-reliance and moral responsibility. Then the people of Israel experienced the promises of big government when they went into Egypt to survive famine. Pharaoh's big government welcomed Israel with promises of plenty and security. In addition to the offer of plenty Pharaoh's government promised to respect the children of Israel's beliefs and leave them alone in the land of Goshen. This big government was so wonderful that even one of their own, Joseph, was a part of Egypt's big government! Surely there was everything to be gained and nothing to be feared by putting faith in this energetic big government. The problem was (and still is) that just because a government intends to do good today does not mean that it will do good tomorrow. After a few generations the once free people of Israel found themselves enslaved to Egypt's big government. If Pharaoh had offered food in exchange for their freedom, the offer would have been rejected. But government seldom encroaches on people's freedom all at once—such bold acts by government would risk an uprising. The best way to enslave a free people is to do it slowly while promising them material betterments "free" from government. This is how the pharaohs gained the enslavement of Israel—without ever risking a revolt.

When God brought Israel out of Egyptian bondage, He gave Israel a simple law by which they were to govern themselves. The Ten Commandments, as we refer to them, were given to Israel after Israel had been delivered from enslavement to Pharaoh's big government in Egypt. Moses and later Joshua ruled in a manner similar to that of the patriarchs. Israel was an extended family, living as a community, under the rule of moral men appointed by God. God established strict rules and requirements of morality for those who were to help Moses in the execution of his governing duties.[1]

The Ten Commandments are not only rules of morality as it relates to men's duties and responsibilities to God, but also rules of morality as it relates to men's duties and responsibilities to each other. The first commandment requires God's people to have no other god before Him—nothing is so important that it comes between moral man and his duty to God. This commandment declares that He is a jealous God. Unfortunately, modern Americans find it difficult to understand that unconditional reverence for and faith in government as the primary solution to social and moral problems can result in the people slowly exchanging faith in God in favor of faith in god-government.[2] This reverence for government is demonstrated by the very small amount of charitable giving by secular humanists, liberals, and nominal socialists. These non-Christians do not give to charity,[2] because their faith is placed in god-government. Such people believe it is the job of government to force people to hand over their money

---

1. See Exodus 18:21-23.
2. See Dixie's Unwelcomed Presence in Rosie O'Donnell's America©, Addendum II.

to government in order for government to take care of the socially downtrodden. Those who control god-government are also jealous and will use all the power and resources (taxes) "we the people" will surrender to fight against god-government's primary competitor—the God of biblical morality.

One of the effects of Adam and Eve breaking God's commandment in the Garden of Eden was that thereafter man would earn his bread by the sweat of his brow—for man to survive he must be engaged in productive labor. The fourth commandment[3] reinforces this truth by declaring in part, "Six days shalt thou labor…" (Exodus 20:9). It is interesting that from this scripture as well as the one in Genesis, it is evident that God has ordained man to be engaged in productive activity. This productive activity results in man acquiring private property—that is, property that belongs to a specific individual. God then warned man, "Thou shalt not steal" (v. 15), and He also issued a warning to man against coveting "anything that is thy neighbor's" (v. 17). It is clear from this passage that: (1) God requires man to be productively employed, (2) man's productivity will result in men holding private property, and (3) God expects His people to respect the property rights of their fellows.

Very often secular humanists, liberals, and nominal socialists attack people who resent government's efforts to extort private property via taxation by claiming that it is immoral to cling to private property when government needs the property to help the disadvantaged. The truth is that using government to acquire another man's property against that man's will is no different than stealing. Government, even when sanctified by a majority vote, cannot turn an otherwise immoral act into a moral act.

When God brought Israel into the Promised Land, He gave them a very limited, decentralized government of judges for the tribes of Israel. But it was not long before the people of Israel began demanding a king. God had already rejected big government (kings and pharaohs) and had provided His people a limited form of government—this fact alone should go a long way in convincing moral people about the dangers of big government. God's warning

---

3. In this book all of the Ten Commandments listed in Exodus 20 were numbered according to the Jewish system of numbering.

about the dangers of a king (i.e., big government of the day) stands the test of time and remains a warning to us today about the dangers of god-government. We find the warning in 1 Samuel:

> And Samuel told all the words of the Lord unto the people who asked of him a king. And he said, This will be the manner of the king who shall reign over you: he will take your sons, and appoint them for himself, for his chariots, and to be his horsemen; and some shall run before his chariots. And he will appoint for himself captains over thousands, and captains over fifties; and will set them to plow his ground, and to reap his harvest, and to make his instruments of war, and instruments of his chariots. And he will take your daughters to be perfumers, and to be cooks, to be bakers. And he will take your fields, and your vineyards, and your olive yards, even the best of them, and give them to his servants. And he will take the tenth of your seed, and of your vineyards, and give to his officers, and to his servants. And he will take your menservants, and your maidservants, and your choicest young men, and your asses, and put them to his work. He will take the tenth of your sheep; and ye shall be his servants. And ye shall cry out in that day because of your king whom ye shall have chosen; and the Lord will not hear you in that day.[4]

Notice that the new government under a king would result in the government of Israel taking away the private property of the people of Israel. The king (government) had no resources of its own. The only way the king could pay the cost of government was by "taking" private property from the productive people. This act of "taking" violates the commandment not to steal, but because the king is doing the stealing, then no one dares to complain—it is hard to stand on principle when the choice is between keeping your private property or keeping your head! It is also instructive for modern readers to understand why the king steals his subjects' private property. The king steals his subjects' private property in order to pay for the loyalty of his supporters—those close to the source of power who have a natural interest in maintaining the *status quo*. The king needs loyal servants (supporters in today's

4. 1 Samuel 8:10-18.

political jargon) because they will be the ones to enforce the king's edits. A loyal court, a loyal police and military, and a loyal religious establishment are all necessary to maintain the king securely in this office. Such things are very costly, but the king does not have to "labor" or earn his keep by the "sweat" of his brow—he merely takes from the productive and gives to those who, thanks to the king's government, are no longer required to labor. The king, his court, his military, and the religious establishment that supports the king all lead parasitic lives. The cost is paid by the productive who must labor to earn enough for the king—who like all government has first claim on productive labor—and then hopefully have enough left over for the productive individual.

The next verse is perhaps the saddest because it reflects the poor judgment of immoral man and the danger that such men represent when they control government or, as in a democracy, when they outvote moral men: "Nevertheless, the people refused to obey the voice of Samuel; and they said, Nay, but we will have a king over us" (v. 19). God has given His people fair warning about the danger of big government. He has given His people precise examples of what happens when people put their trust in god-government. Yet, in spite of all the warnings, His people too often look to government to solve their problems and end up with more government, more taxes to pay for more government, less personal freedom, and a nation whose official stance is to deny traditional moral values.

The kings of Israel—man-inspired government—taught the nation to sin. Patriarchs did not teach Israel to sin, nor did the limited government under the judges teach Israel to sin. It was government under kings that institutionalized sin; government "normalized" sin and made it socially acceptable and eventually turned the cruel force of government against moral leaders who opposed unrighteousness. This is to be expected any time uncontrolled power is placed in the hands of fallen men. The tendency of man to seek selfish pleasures and avoid "labor" is only magnified when men are entrusted with the power of government. The saintly patriot-prophet Jeremiah lamented the evil that corrupt kings and corrupt religious leaders of his day had brought upon Judah. Again and again God warned the people; again and again God punished his people; but again and again fallen man, empowered by government, refused to heed God's warnings.

When government needs "moral" authority for its immoral acts it can always count on false prophets and corrupt religious leaders to come to the defense of government. The book of Matthew contains a warning from Jesus about false teachers: "Beware of false prophets, who come to you in sheep's clothing, but inwardly they are ravening wolves."[5] Why would "religious" leaders support a corrupt government? It is because the religious hierarchy is actually a part of the system of government—it supports the *status quo,* and government rewards the religious hierarchy with special privileges. In modern America the opportunity for such an arrangement has been greatly reduced because the founding fathers made sure the Federal government could not establish an official religion that would be beholding to government. Unfortunately, much of the work formerly done for government in prior times by the religious hierarchy is now done by the liberal media[6] and government schools.

Some Christians misread Jesus' command, "Render to Caesar the things that are Caesar's, and to God the things that are God's" (Mark 12:17). The New Testament is clear in its instruction for Christians to obey those in authority. But it is also equally clear that when it comes to the question "Should we obey man or God?" the answer is always to follow God's teachings in matters of faith and morality. The operative part of Jesus' command cited above is to render unto Caesar things that belong to the realm of government, obey legitimate laws enacted by government, but to render only those things that rightfully belong to government, especially if government intervenes into the realm of moral principles.

Man was created perfect by God, but man sinned against God, and sin entered into the world. As a fallen creature, man is in need of redemption. If left to his own devices, man will always tend to follow the evil inclination of his heart. Government run by fallen man is therefore corrupted as a result of man's sinful nature. Fallen man will eventually use government's supra-personal force to benefit those holding the power of government and those with

---

5. Matthew 7:15.

6. See James Ronald Kennedy and Walter Donald Kennedy, *Why Not Freedom!* (Gretna, LA: Pelican Publishing Company, 1994), pp. 159-67.

close ties to government. The exercise of the force of government by fallen man tends to corrupt the morals of society. The larger the government the greater harm it will eventually do to society's morals. God has given us clear warnings about the dangers of big government. Historically, and rationally, the only way to maintain a moral community is to keep the corrosive power of government at a minimum. Israel failed to heed God's warning, and the result of its longing after big government was moral decay, spiritual degeneracy, and national enslavement. Moral decay and spiritual degeneracy (sin) always lead to loss of liberty. This was true for Israel in the Old Testament, and it will also be true for America today. The great question for moral Americans is how can we avoid a similar fate?

Section II

God's Principles of Limited Government

4

Self-Ownership— First Principle of Human Liberty

Principle Number 1: *Liberty is based on the principle of self-ownership and personal accountability. Human liberty is indispensible for the promotion, development, and maintenance of a prosperous, peaceful and moral society.*

Self-Ownership

The first principle of human liberty in a moral community is that liberty is based on the concept that mature individuals are personally responsible for themselves. An individual is not the property of the village chief, a powerful lord, a wealthy business person, religious authority, or government. The best description of this term "self-ownership" is one little heard today: "Individual responsibility and personal accountability." Philosophers and writers have attributed the origins of this basic freedom to natural law, natural rights, or an indisputable gift from God.[1] Philosophical debates are not important for the purpose of this study. The important fact is that any form of government, especially mass democracy, that does not begin with the principle of self-ownership will eventually use its power to infringe upon and ultimately destroy individual freedom and liberty.

Self-ownership requires that each individual in society respect the person and property of other individuals. Most atheists recognize that "Thou shall not steal" is a good rule. If we assume

---

1. Self-ownership and protection of property rights are not an exclusive element of the Protestant work ethic. Henry of Ghent, a great Catholic master at the University of Paris in the thirteenth century, defended property rights on the grounds of individual self-ownership. Pope Leo XIII noted that property rights were "sacred and inviolable" because they were a "natural right." Thomas E. Woods, Jr., *The Church and the Market: A Catholic Defense of the Free Market* (New York: Lexington Books, 2005), p. 195.

that all individuals own themselves, then this principle precludes acts of theft or oppression by one individual against another individual. The same is true of groups of individuals stealing or oppressing other groups. The fact that the oppressing group is larger and the oppressed group is smaller in no way changes the fact that oppression or theft is a violation of the principle of self-ownership. Oppression is not sanctified by a majority vote— the evil nature of oppression is not altered even if the evil act is approved by a majority vote in a democracy.

Self-Ownership and Property Rights

Self-ownership is the highest form of property rights. All other rights are derived from this principle. For example, if a free individual works to convert a natural resource not owned by another individual, a stone for example, into a tool, then the stone that was free to anyone who picked it up now becomes the personal property of the worker who used his skills and labor to transform the stone into a useful tool. Because the individual owns himself he has the full and complete right to the fruit of his labors. This right to property is so important that men everywhere and at all times have formed themselves into communities to protect themselves from the threat of thieves and brigands who would steal the fruit of the workingman's labor. The right to the fruits of one's labor is the key element that motivates highly skilled and intuitive individuals (entrepreneurs) to seek ways to improve their lot in life, and in so doing they make life better for everyone in society. For example; Bill Gates transformed an entire industry in which computers were large mainframes owned by huge corporations and unknowable to the average person in society. Today, personal computers have become a standard household item, the Internet has expanded our ability to communicate, and typewriters have become museum artifacts. Yes, Bill Gates (and a substantial number of his compatriots and competitors) became very wealthy in the process. But that wealth was obtained by providing consumers something they wanted. The increase in social wealth (just think about the number of people who now own personal computers) would not have been possible in a society that did not respect the entrepreneur's property rights.

A society that fails to respect property rights will remain primitive and impoverished. A society that respects property rights will become prosperous. Notice that when a nation follows God's will, that nation prospers—righteousness does indeed exalt a nation! The great tragedy seen throughout modern history is that when a free society becomes prosperous, certain elements within that society become envious of those highly skilled and intuitive individuals who "have more than they need" and will begin to seek ways to "legally" steal the wealth of the successful members of society—and not just the highly successful members, but all who are productive. While envy and covetousness is the primary driver of such men, they hide their true motives behind high-sounding words such as "compassion, fairness, nondiscrimination, an even playing field, and equality." In a democratic society legalizing theft is done via government action sanctioned by a majority vote.

Self-Ownership and Self-Sufficiency

Self-ownership is essential if people are to become self-sufficient. Self-sufficiency does not imply that free individuals are social hermits, nor does it imply that the free individual does not need other people. Man is a social being. We need and generally seek the community of our fellows. What self-sufficiency implies is that the individual takes responsibility for the care and keeping of himself—other people will not be forced by government to bear his burden. Self-sufficiency or individual responsibility is a prerequisite to being free and enjoying the benefits of liberty. This sense of individual responsibility will produce the following characteristics in an individual: (1) the concept that the individual is solely responsible for his actions, (2) the concept that the individual must accept the consequences for his actions or inactions, and (3) the knowledge that the individual will not be allowed to shift his responsibility to society if he does not take care of his own needs. The concept of taking responsibility for one's action coupled with the knowledge that society is not going to "pull one's irons out of the fire" is the hallmark of a healthy and free society. An individual (or even a whole group of people) who by his own effort cannot provide for himself is not free. People in bondage, be they prisoners, slaves, or government dependents, look to others for their basic needs. Those who rely upon society for their support (food, shelter, health care, etc.) are not free—they are in reality vassals, serfs, or slaves.

Self-Ownership and Personal Accountability

No one had to remind early American pioneers that they were accountable for their action or inaction. American pioneers who brought civilization to the frontier did not expect society to provide them a "social safety net" to protect them from bad decisions or poor planning. They did not look to government to provide housing, food, or support for their children. There was no governmentally provided aid to dependent children, "free" health care, food stamps, or governmental legal services to secure group rights. In early America the individual was responsible for taking care of himself. This principle was once proudly embraced by a people who took great pride in maintaining their personal freedom and independence. These people knew intuitively that once an individual begins to rely on others or government to take care of him, that individual surrenders self-ownership and slowly becomes a slave to those providing his sustenance. The tragic result of America's abandonment of the principles of personal accountability and individual responsibility is nowhere more evident than in America's inner-city ghettos.

The good intentions of nominal socialists[2] have created a culture of dependency in America's inner cities. The intention was to use government to give the downtrodden a "hand up." But because government social workers cannot discriminate between the "deserving and non-deserving" poor[3], they merely established unending giveaway programs. Before long in the inner-city ghetto working to support oneself became less attractive than living off the public dole, especially since it had been established that society owed this "aid" to the downtrodden—public welfare became a right. Of course it was not lost on liberal politicians that by giving an ever increasing amount of public funds to certain groups these

2. See the definition of "nominal socialists" in the introduction.

3. "Deserving poor" is a term used by private (usually religious-based) charities in the late nineteenth century to describe individuals who through no fault of their own found themselves destitute and with the assistance of temporary aid could once again join society as self-supporting citizens. The "non-deserving poor" were those who evidenced an intention to live parasitically off the charity of society. These individuals were excluded from the rolls of charity.

groups would be indebted to the politicians and would repay the debt by casting their votes *en masse* for liberal candidates. Star Parker who, by her own efforts, raised herself out of inner-city poverty, clearly described the stark reality of government interventions that destroyed people's desire to take care of themselves by "selling" their votes to liberal politicians.

> Men and women like this minister and his willing accomplices in the liberal establishment are involved in the slave trade, as surely as if they had put the chains on the people themselves. We work the ghettos instead of the fields, dutifully putting "massa" back in the Senate or House of Representatives, so they'll keep those compassionate benefits coming. They get power; we get a free ride. Everybody wins. Except we don't. The results have been disastrous.[4]

The sad fact is that politicians, the ruling elite who control government, do not want people to become self-reliant! Politicians know that once former recipients become self-reliant they no longer need the "free" services provided by parasitic politicians. What is even worst for the politicians is that once the former welfare recipients become self-reliant individuals they begin to recognize politicians for the parasites they actually are and stop voting for those political parasites who want to extort OPM.

The combination of irrational good intentions of nominal socialists and the political greed of the ruling elite has produced a government in which taxes derived from the productive element of society are used to buy votes from political parasites. All of this is done to the detriment of those whom the good intentions of nominal socialists had supposedly meant to help and to the detriment of the productive element whose ability and incentive to be productive have been severely hampered.

Self-Ownership and the Family

While a free society, that is a society that accepts the principle of self-ownership, is composed of free individuals, these individuals

---

4. Star Parker, *Uncle Sam's Plantation* (Nashville, TN: WND Books, 2003), pp. 52-53.

are not born and raised in isolation, nor do they live out their lives in isolation. The wholeness of an individual is brought about in community with others. The basic element of the community is the family. Husband and wife create new life and, by so doing, add living resources to the community. Apart from the very essential spiritual side of the family—companionship, love, and a sense of belonging and owing a duty to a long line of kinsmen stretching back into the distant past—the family also acts as a social insurance policy. The family provides its members a balanced perspective on both the past and the future. Through the family the present has a direct link to the past—to those who have gone before and are now departed from this realm—and provides the means to safely accept the uncertainties of the future. The family does not end with the husband, wife, and their children. The family extends outward to the extended family composed of grandparents, uncles, aunts, and cousins. All adult members of the extended family have a duty to take care of themselves and their immediate family (often referred to as the nuclear family) and to come to the aid of members of the extended family should such a need arise.

"Kith and kin" is an old Scotch-Irish term that describes how communities would work together for mutual aid and protection. "Kin" referred to the extended family, while "kith" referred to those families that while not related by blood were close friends who knew each other and knew they could call upon the other for help in times of crisis or danger. Strong and healthy families, extended families, and close friends are an essential element in creating and maintaining free and moral local communities. Free and moral local communities are the essential elements in creating a free society. The labor and productive enterprise of individuals produce private property necessary to sustain and nourish the family. Families create moral communities, and moral communities create a moral society. None of this would be possible if it were not for the self-owning individual creating private property. Thus, we see the importance of property rights that are not derived from a constitution crafted by sly politicians but that arise from the inalienable right of self-ownership.

Self-Ownership Versus the Ruling Elite
Unfortunately, sly politicians know that communities composed of strong and self-reliant families pose a significant barrier to the

envy and greed of politicians and those closely connected to the political ruling elite. Politicians know that people who rely upon themselves and their local community have very little need for a powerful political leader, government bureaucrats, and legions of regulators who promise to provide for the needs of the poor, the ignorant, the downtrodden, or the oppressed masses.

Since the Great Depression, American government has become the enemy of the family. Legislation, touted as socially necessary, has in fact lead to the destruction of traditional family ties and mutually accepted responsibilities. Since the 1930s families have become more and more dependent upon government for the social security that was formerly provided by the family and community. This has worked to the great advantage of politicians who use private property extorted from working men and women via taxes and inflation[5] to buy votes by promising certain advantages and payments to specific voting blocs. Who in America today is foolish enough to believe that the rate that entrenched politicians win re-election is due to the good job they are doing protecting the private property of working men and women! As the family becomes less important as a social unit—government moves into the vacuum it created to replace the family. As individuals become dependent on government—the once free (self-owning) individual becomes a government dependent, then a government serf, and eventually a slave in a completely socialized society where neither individual nor family is important—the state becomes all, and "we the people" become expendable fodder.

5. See James Ronald Kennedy, *Reclaiming Liberty* (Gretna, LA: Pelican Publishing Company, 2005), p. 126.

5

What Constitutes a Legitimate Government?

Principle Number 2: *For government to be legitimate it must be founded on the free, unfettered, and qualified consent of the governed.*

Do Free People Need Government?

Before we can determine the parameters of legitimate government we must first establish whether or not government is even necessary. As we saw in the previous chapter, self-ownership is the highest form of property rights. From this right flow all other property rights. The commandment "Thou shall not steal" is in fact an ancient and divine reflection of the importance of property rights. If man lived a solitary existence, then theft would not be an issue. But because humans are social beings, human passions such as envy, covetousness, and greed make it necessary to have some way to protect property rights.

John C. Calhoun was an American political philosopher of the nineteenth century—a man who distinguished himself as U.S. vice president and U.S. senator from South Carolina. Calhoun noted that human government is universally necessary and is an "incontestable fact"[1] He wrote that man is so constituted that he is always found in society with other men. The fact that man is a social being also presents a problem for property rights. Because, according to Calhoun, man feels his personal wants, needs, and desires more keenly than he feels the need to protect and promote the wants, needs, and desires of others, man has the strong tendency to act selfishly within the social setting. The simple truth that Calhoun enunciated is that humans tend to be in conflict with

---

1. John C. Calhoun, "A Disquisition on Government," quoted in, *The Works of John C. Calhoun*, Vol. I. (New York: D. Appleton and Company, MDCCCLIV), p. 1.

each other because men feel more keenly things that affect them directly (personally) than those things that affect them indirectly (through the pain, distress, anger, disappointment of others in society). This tendency of men to be in conflict with each other gives rise to the necessity for some controlling instrumentality or government. According to Calhoun:

> It follows, then, that man is so constituted, that government is necessary to the existence of society, and society to his existence and the perfection of his faculties. It follows, also, that government has its origin in this twofold constitution of his nature; the sympathetic or social feelings constituting the remote—and the individual or direct, the proximate cause.[2]

It was obvious to Calhoun and his generation Who was the author of man's inherent desire to be in society with other humans—"the Infinite Being, the Creator of all...His infinite wisdom and goodness...He has assigned the social and political state."[3] This desire to be in a social state gave rise to the need for government—a controlling element that would prevent the stronger from oppressing the property rights of weaker people. But Calhoun warned that this very government that was created by man to protect the property of people in society had within it a very strong "tendency to disorder and abuse of its powers."[4] He then asked a question that has troubled Americans from the very beginning of the country:

> How can those who are invested with the powers of government be prevented from employing them, as the means of aggrandizing themselves instead of using them to protect and preserve society?[5]

The primary function of government—indeed the only legitimate function for government is to protect citizens' property rights. Due to man's inherent tendency to be in conflict with others—or to

2. Ibid., 4, 5.
3. Ibid., 6, 7.
4. Ibid., 7.
5. Ibid., 8.

feel the desire for personal improvement more than the desire for the improvement of society in general—man needs government to protect the many who are capable of restraining their passions of greed, envy, etc., from those few who refuse to control such negative passions. Calhoun demonstrated to his generation that government, composed of fallen creatures (sinful men), has a strong tendency to become corrupt and controlled by a few powerful men who use the power of government to oppress those who have no governmental power. Thus, "good" government devolves into a tyranny worse than that which it was originally created to prevent. Government is needed, but it is also very dangerous. As George Washington stated, "Government is not elegance, it is not reason, it is like fire, a dangerous servant but a fearful master."[6]

What Is the Origin of Legitimate Government?

The quest to determine the source of legitimate government was a key topic of discussion for many early European political philosophers. The answer was succinctly penned by Thomas Jefferson in the American colonies' Declaration of Independence: "...Governments are instituted among Men, deriving their just powers from the consent of the governed." Early Americans, who believed in personal freedom, christened their new government with the declaration that the only way a government could be legitimate—that is, the only way it could justly require the loyalty of free men—was for that government to rule with the consent (permission) of the people.

The idea that government derived its right to rule from the consent of the people was a radical and revolutionary idea in 1776. At that time it was accepted that the king ruled as a result of an appointment from God. It was accepted that the government of that day ruled the people by "Divine Right." It is important to note who accepted and enforced this logic of government. Divine right of government was accepted by the "powers that be," "the ruling elite," the politically correct crowd of that time who controlled government and those close to government who derived great value

---

6. George Washington, as cited in, Edward G. Griffin, *The Fearful Master* (Boston: Western Islands Publishers, 1964), p. ii.

from their relationship with that government. The ruling elite at that time derived great wealth as a result of their loyalty to the idea that God appointed certain men to rule the rest of mankind. It was a time of absolute power held by kings, queens, the Royal Court, and those closely associated with the monarchy. By their way of thinking, and remember their way of thinking was very profitable for those holding power, God appoints men to high stations and low stations in life, and such arrangements may never change. Thomas Jefferson would later castigate such thinking when he declared that no man is born booted and spurred to ride over his fellow man.[7] This is why Thomas Jefferson placed in the Declaration of Independence the American idea that "all men are created equal." Not equal in height, weight, talents, motivations, or intelligence, but equal before the law and before God. Free men stand before the law as equals; no man is allowed preference before the law because of the accident of his birth, nor is another man relegated to a position of less protection from the law due to the accident of his birth.

How Is Consent Obtained?

Most Americans would answer the question of "How is consent to government obtained?" by stating that when we vote we are by implication giving our consent to the government that is a result of the election. This is a logical but very dangerous answer! Let us suppose that we live in a democracy that is composed of 50 percent Christians and 50 percent Muslims. On election day an illness attacks the Christian community, and slightly fewer of the Christian voters go to the polls while all of the Muslim voters go to the polls. The obvious outcome of this democratically held election is a new president and Congress dominated by Muslim politicians. This new government immediately (in a great rush, without allowing time for the opposition and the ordinary citizens to read the new legislation) enacts a law that no Christian symbols, relics, books, or prayers can be displayed in any public area, but makes no mention of Muslim

---

7. "...the mass of mankind has not been born with saddles on their backs, nor a favored few booted and spurred, ready to ride them..." *The Life and Selected Writings of Thomas Jefferson*, edited by Adrienne Koch and William Peden, (New York: The Modern Library, 1944), pp. 729-30.

symbols, relics, books, or prayers. Did the Christian minority give their consent to this government by merely participating in the democratic election process?

John C. Calhoun warned Americans about the dangers posed by a democratically elected government in which the numerical majority could use the force of government to oppress the rights of the numerical minority. Calhoun warned that in such a democratic government there would come a time when those who obtained their wealth or subsistence from government would compose the numerical majority, and this numerical majority would always vote for those politicians who promised to tax or otherwise exploit the numerical minority in order to fund the wealth transfer from the numerical minority to the numerical majority. In the early 1840s Calhoun had already identified the fatal flaw in all mass democracies—the electoral tipping point in which the nonproductive element outvotes the productive element and by gaining control of government uses government's monopoly on the use of force to compel the productive element to transfer its wealth to the nonproductive element. This is the end stage of all mass democracies—American or otherwise—the stage in which government becomes the instrument for legalized looting of the dwindling, law-abiding, moral, productive element. Remember, all of this is accomplished in the most democratic fashion—the power of the ballot box is used to establish a dictatorship of the numerical majority. As far as the numerical minority is concerned, it matters not at all whether or not this dictatorship was established by armed force or by the overwhelming power of the democratic ballot box. It should also be remembered that the dictatorships of Adolf Hitler and Benito Mussolini were a result of democratic elections!

Most people are born into a society with an established government. It is very rare that people are required to meet and give their consent to the formation of a new government. As a result of being born into a society with an established government, consent to that government is presumed. Voting is a form, but by no means the only nor the most important form, of consent.

How Do Free People Protect Consent?

How do free people protect consent once given or presumed? To believe that once consent is given it remains forever valid not only for the lifetime of the ones giving consent but also for everyone subsequently born into that society makes void the very principle of consent of the governed. Consent to be governed is not unqualified! That means that if a citizen gives his consent to be governed today, but tomorrow government becomes oppressive of his rights, he has the right to withdraw his consent. John Locke, the seventeenth-century political philosopher whose writings greatly influenced Thomas Jefferson, described this right as a legitimate means of escape from oppressive government.[8] John Milton, the seventeenth-century Christian author of *Paradise Lost*, also described how citizens would no longer be required to maintain their loyalty to a government that had grown tyrannical.[9] But withdrawing consent (seceding) from one government and forming a new one is a rather radical solution and should not be undertaken unless no other alternative is left—of course, the alternative to passively submit to tyranny is always an alternative, but not one acceptable to free and moral people. In the words of the Declaration of Independence, "Prudence, indeed, will dictate that Governments long established should not be changed for light and transient causes...." When the American colonies seceded from their union with Great Britain,[10] it was after long and diligent but unsuccessful efforts to maintain their rights as Englishmen. The loss of an election, for example, is not sufficient reason to withdraw consent. But the continued oppression of the numerical minority at the hands of a government controlled by an unjust or immoral numerical majority would give rise to the American right to withdraw consent—an act known as secession. But did America's founding fathers create a government that had no means, other than secession, to protect the numerical minority from the encroachments of a government controlled by the numerical majority? What means other than immediate secession

8. See Consent of the Governed—Key to Liberty, by Walter Donald Kennedy, Addendum III.

9. John Milton, as cited in, James Ronald Kennedy and Walter Donald Kennedy, *The South Was Right!* (Gretna, LA: Pelican Publishing Company, 1994), pp. 185-93.

10. James R. Kennedy and Walter D. Kennedy, *Was Jefferson Davis Right?* (Gretna, LA: Pelican Publishing Company, 1998), p. 58.

did our founding fathers provide under the original American system of constitutionally limited Federalism?

The Sovereign State—America's Defender of Minority Rights

Ask the average American what type of government the founding fathers created, and the answer you are most likely to get is that the founding fathers created a democracy. The answer would not only be wrong, it would be dangerously wrong! As we have already discussed, a mass democracy will always evolve (devolve?) into a system of spoils wherein the numerical majority will use the power of the government that they control to loot the wealth of the numerical minority. By way of reiteration—the wealth looted from the numerical minority is a violation of their property rights. Government, in a mass democracy, is eventually perverted from its role of protecting the property rights of individuals into a means of systematically extorting the property of some for the benefit of those who control government and those who are closely associated with the ruling elite.

The founding fathers created a constitutional republic of republics. Each sovereign state, free and independent states according to the Articles of Confederation that preceded the Constitution of 1789, on behalf of the citizens of their respective state, voluntarily delegated (as opposed to surrendered) certain and specific rights to the new Federal government created by the Constitution, while reserving all rights not *specifically* delegated to their new agent, the Federal government. Under this new government each member state is a free, independent, and sovereign state. In this regard, each state in the American Union is a free, independent, and sovereign republic in all areas of government except those areas in which the sovereign state, acting on behalf of and by the instructions of the people of their respective state, delegated (not surrendered) to their new agent, the Federal government.

The people of each sovereign state compose the sovereign community within their respective state. The consent of "we the people" who compose the sovereign community within the state is the source of authority for our state's government. In other words, in the original American republic of republics the sovereign state acquires its legitimacy from the consent of the citizens who make up the sovereign community within their respective state. Therefore, original authority, legitimacy, or sovereignty belongs to the states (not the Federal government), and delegated and specific authority for the Federal government is derived from and by the permission of the sovereign states. The founding fathers saw this arrangement as the ultimate means to protect the numerical minority in small states from the oppressions of the numerical majority who make up the populations of the larger states. The founding fathers feared a time in which certain populations in certain larger states would league together to form a majority voting bloc, gain control of the Federal government, and use that government to benefit themselves at the expense of the numerical minority in smaller states.

At the time of the debates on the Constitution of 1789 some who supported a strong federal government argued that the founding fathers provided a written constitution that limited the role of the federal government, and that this constitution, in and of itself, would provide adequate protection for the numerical minority. After all, even if a group gained control of the federal government, the harm they could do would be limited because the role of the federal government was very limited. Unfortunately, time has demonstrated the folly of this argument.

The classic, and equally incorrect, argument in favor of a strong federal government (and against state sovereignty) is the fact that the Constitution created a system of checks and balances in which one arm of the Federal government (executive, legislative, or judicial, that is, the Supreme Court) would provide a check on the excesses of the other arms of government. This sets up the classic question of "Who shall guard the guards?" If the numerical majority elects a majority in Congress, elects the president, and nominates a majority on the Supreme Court, what is the likelihood of the Federal government acting, ruling, or legislating against the interests of the numerical majority who control the Federal government?

The founding fathers created a system composed of a written constitution with specific and enumerated powers delegated to the Federal government, and they sought to limit the excesses of the Federal government by creating a system of checks and balances within the Federal system. But this was not and is not the final word as to the limits of Federal authority. The founding fathers recognized that the ultimate authority for the Federal government arose from "we the people" of the sovereign community acting within our respective states. The founding fathers knew that the sovereign state would continue to act as the ultimate bulwark against acts of oppression by the Federal government against "we the people" in our respective sovereign states. If this protection had not been established the anti-federalists, who were a majority when the Constitution of 1789 was submitted to the sovereign states for their ratification or rejection, would not have agreed to ratification of the Constitution.

The loss of the protection provided to free people of the states in the current American Federal system has given rise to the supremacy of the current Federal government, destruction of constitutional safeguards, unlimited encroachments of rights originally reserved to the sovereign states (for example; the right of the state to decide when human life begins), the legalized looting of the property rights of the productive element of society for the benefit of nonproductive elements, and other acts destructive of personal liberty too numerous to enumerate in this short book.[11]

The only legitimate government is that government that has the active consent of the governed. In the American system, consent of the sovereign community is granted to their respective states. The states then are the source of the delegated authority exercised by the Federal government. Under the original system of constitutionally limited federalism the sovereign state acted as the final arbiter of whether or not an act of the Federal government was constitutional—whether an act of the Federal government was in fact legitimate, requiring the citizen to comply. Under the original American republic of republics if the Federal government ruled, for example, that the Holy Bible would not be allowed in a schoolroom, the sovereign state could, at the behest of its citizens, interpose its sovereign authority between the onerous Federal edict and the people of that state. In a word it was called nullification. By nullifying an onerous act of the Federal government the sovereign state on behalf of its citizens withdrew their consent to be governed by the Federal government as it related to and only as it related to the specific area of conflict. Nullification provided Americans the ability to withdraw their consent without destroying the government. It then allowed for a cooling down period in which both

---

11. For more detail, see James Ronald Kennedy and Walter Donald Kennedy, *Why Not Freedom!* (Gretna, LA: Pelican Publishing Company, 1994), pp. 63-240.

sides could seek a permanent solution to the controversy at hand. It was a way to preserve both personal liberty and the legitimate union established by the Constitution.

6

The Inherently Oppressive
Nature of Government

Principle Number 3: *Human government, regardless of its size or form, is inherently oppressive of human liberty.*

Whose Money Is It—the Tax Payer's or the Tax Collector's?

Too many moral, law-abiding Americans have the mistaken notion that the government has a natural almost Divine Right to take any amount of a citizen's property, usually by way of taxation, that government finds necessary and proper for its political purposes. Forget about nominal socialists (liberals) and actual socialists; they actually believe that it is the role of all governments to use any means necessary to bring about social justice—and of course it is social justice as they choose to define it. This liberal/socialist collectivist attitude precludes respect for any of the limitations imposed on government by an "outdated" written constitution. Beyond this group of liberals and nominal socialists is a large group of moral, law-abiding, taxpaying Americans who readily and unquestioningly grant to government the right to expropriate any amount of their personal property as long as the government can muster a majority vote in an election and then pass the tax law through the legislative process. How have once freedom-loving Americans succumbed to such fawning behavior toward the tax collector? This is especially depressing when one recalls that the American Revolution was essentially a tax revolt—a revolt against taxes in 1776 that would be miniscule when compared to the level of taxation Americans routinely tolerate today.[1] Back then, Americans looked upon the forced removal of personal property for what it was—the step-by-step destruction of the free man's ability to remain free.

---

1. James Ronald Kennedy, *Reclaiming Liberty* (Gretna, LA: Pelican Publishing Company, 2005), pp. 163-83.

Taxation or Legalized Theft?

Government agents have the ability to do things to citizens that, were the agents not part of the government, they would be seized by the local law enforcement service and thrown into jail. But a government agent can come into citizens' home, the place they work, or the places they do business, and tell them just how much of their money they may keep and how much they must hand over to the government—and he can do it with perfect immunity.

As previously noted, the first principle of freedom is based on the concept of self-ownership, and from that right is derived the right to own the fruits of one's labors. The only legitimate role of the Federal government is to protect the national borders from foreign invasion, assure free trade among those sovereign states that voluntarily elect to be a part of the national confederation (republic of republics), and protect or adjudicate disputes regarding property rights involving citizens from different states or adjudicate disputes between citizens of a state and the Federal government. The state's primary responsibility is to serve as a defense against the encroachments of the Federal government upon the rights reserved to the states and the people thereof. The state's secondary responsibility is to protect its citizens from the violence of domestic criminals. All taxation beyond that required to accomplish these goals amounts to an attempt by the ruling elite to legalize theft via taxation.[2] Taxation beyond the level needed to sustain minimal government[3] is an act of gradual enslavement. The taxpayer no longer has the right to keep the fruits of his labors but is compelled to perform "involuntary servitude" on behalf to the ruling elite who set the requirements for how much "free" time the tax slave may

---

2. In addition to taxation, government also uses its ability to create money and credit out of thin air as a means of financing its projects and giveaway schemes. The cost is ultimately paid by the consumer in the form of inflation. See James Ronald Kennedy, *Reclaiming Liberty*, pp. 127-45.

3. The authors advocate a total taxation rate (local, state, and Federal) of no more than 10 percent of true Gross Domestic Product (computed without counting government spending as a contributor to the GDP). And for government to be considered free the total taxation rate must be always trending downward. James Ronald Kennedy, *Reclaiming Liberty*, p. 164.

have and how much forced time he must provide his governmental masters. What alchemy or sorcerer's spell have the ruling elite used to compel American citizens to endure the greatest tax load in American history plus an immeasurable national debt and a proven record of governmental social and economic failures?

Taxation—An Act of Patriotism or Nationalism?

America's ruling elite have discovered that patriotic Americans—those moral citizens who obey the law, pay their taxes, and try to make a productive and positive contribution to society—these Americans will bear almost any burden provided they think it is somehow a part of their patriotic duty. If the government decides it wants to wage a war to secure certain privileges for favored corporations, then all it need do is rattle the sabers and patriotic citizens will pledge their treasure and blood to "defend" national interest. If government needs more money to bail out its friends in the banking and financing industry (as it did in the late 1980s during the savings and loan crises and most recently in 2008 and 2009) all it need do is remind patriotic citizens about their duty to help "their" government rescue the nation's economy. The problem is that Americans no longer understand the difference between patriotism and nationalism.

Adolf Hitler declared that he was not a patriot but a nationalist. There is more than a mere academic distinction between these terms.

> We have seen that while true patriotism is defensive, nationalism is aggressive; patriotism is the love of a particular land, with its particular traditions; nationalism is the love of something less tangible, of the myth of a "people," justifying everything, a political and ideological substitute for religion...[4]

Patriotism looks inward to community and local traditions, whereas nationalism looks outward for worlds to conquer. Patriotism sees other people as possible trading partners with whom to engage in voluntary exchange—an exchange in which

---

4. John Lukacs, *Democracy and Populism: Fear and Hatred* (New Haven and London: Yale University Press, 2005), pp. 71-72.

both sides improve and maximize their wealth. Nationalism sees other people simultaneously as a potential threat and as a source for exploitation. Nationalists seek a relationship in which their nation gains advantage at the expense of other people's nations. Most Christians are very comfortable with the notion of patriotism but not as comfortable with the notion of nationalism. Patriots have no problem following the Lord's commandment "Do unto others as you would have them do unto you," but nationalists are, by the very nature of nationalism, forced to violate this simple commandment.

In modern America no distinction is made between patriotism and nationalism. Much of this is due to the propaganda efforts of the government during both world wars plus the natural tendency of conservatives and anti-communists during the Cold War to identify support for national security with patriotism. During the presidential terms of George W. Bush many moral conservatives who truly believed in limited government were more than willing to grant the "conservative" president terrible powers to invade privacy and conduct torture all in the patriotic name of national security. America's ruling elite (both Democrats and Republicans) know how to manipulate the American people's bedrock sense of patriotism in order to secure an expansion of government at the expense of personal liberty and the continued exploitation of property rights and private wealth. For generations—regardless of which political party is in power or whether the political philosophy of conservatives or liberals is in vogue—government has increased, and personal liberty has diminished.

Government Creates Class Division in Society

Contemporary American politicians are well known for their promises to "bring us together as a people" or to "pass laws to heal the divisions in our society," yet somehow each election cycle these same politicians, or their electoral opponents, come back with the same promises. One can only assume that their first plan to "heal and bring us together" must have failed—yet we re-elect them, or someone just like them, each election cycle. The truth is that politicians both create and exploit the divisions in our society.

Trade between individuals encourages mutual respect and the building of permanent friendly relations. Government's role in this case is to stay out of the way and allow free individuals to operate in the free market for their mutual advantage. But this would leave politicians "out in the cold" with limited opportunity to personally gain from the redistribution of other people's money. Politicians enjoy using OPM to fund government programs or projects (usually completed by contractors or developers who have made substantial contributions to key politicians' campaign finance committees). These government programs and projects provide politicians photo opportunities—always helpful close to election time—and an opportunity to indirectly, and sometimes directly, repay those whose financial support was instrumental in the politicians wining their political power.

While trade in the free market brings people together, political action tends to divide people into those who benefit from any given government policy, programs, or projects, and those who via taxation are forced to pay for government policy, programs, or projects. Politicians find this very useful because those who benefit from government programs, special interest groups such as welfare recipients for example, tend to be well organized politically even though they represent a smaller number of people. Because the special interest group is politically organized it can be counted on to turn out members of the special interest group *en masse* to vote for the politician who provided OPM to support the needs and wants of the special interest group. On the other hand, those who pay for government programs, taxpayers, while more numerous, are not politically organized and therefore have little if any voice in the legislative political decision-making process. This is because the increase in taxes to pay for additional government programs is a relatively small increase on the individual's tax burden. This makes it extremely difficult for the productive individual to justify taking time away from his busy work schedule to become politically involved during each session of the legislature. At best all the taxpayer can do is faithfully go to the polls on election day and attempt to vote for the lesser of two evils. The votes from special interest groups are unified for their favored candidate, the one giving them the most OPM, while the votes of taxpayers are fragmented. Though smaller in numbers, politicians know they can count on the votes of special interest groups. In America's mass democracy special interest groups and politicians always win, while the unorganized taxpayer (also known as the forgotten man) is always the loser.

Nominal socialists and other bleeding-heart liberals love to proclaim that they want to bring people together—but in reality their favored programs actually divide citizens into two camps, those who gain wealth without earning it, and those who earn wealth but then must surrender it to those who do not deserve it. Karl Marx could not have designed a better class-conflict scenario.

Government's Role as an Oppressor of the Forgotten Man

Government cannot create wealth. There has never been in the history of man a governmental system capable of creating wealth. Wealth is created by private individuals engaging in voluntary exchange. Because government has no source of wealth to obtain the funds it needs even to carry out its legitimate functions, it must take wealth from the productive element of society. This is usually accomplished by taxation. Taxation takes private property away for the productive citizen. This act alone, even when it is done for a legitimate reason, is a violation of the property rights of the individual. To avoid becoming a tyranny, government must perform only those functions absolutely necessary and obtain the consent from those who must bear the burden of taxation. The founding fathers sought to avoid a national government and thereby keep most governmental functions at the local level where local patriotic citizens could keep a close eye on the workings of their elected leaders.

7

Minimal Government—The Least Oppressive Form of Government

Principle Number 4: *All governments are oppressive of liberty with a strong tendency toward tyranny; therefore, to protect liberty human government must be minimal.*

What Kind of Government Should Man Establish?

Man is a social being. Man is normally found in a social setting. An individual who prefers to exist alone in the condition of a hermit is viewed as an oddity by most in society. Yet this natural desire of man for the companionship of his fellows gives rise to conflict. The origin or cause of a very substantial part of human conflict (if not all) is explained in Christian theology by the fact that man is a fallen creature. Man is inherently sinful and in need of divine redemption. For example, the human passions of greed, envy, and covetousness tend to give rise to human conflict. Therefore some form of human government is needed to protect property rights and to peacefully adjudicate conflicts between individuals. The question is not "Does man need human government?" but "What type of human government does man need?"

America's First Free Government

By the time of the Revolutionary War (circa 1776) most Americans had rejected the notion that a specific form of government is of divine origin. The notion of the Divine Right of Kings was very useful for the ruling elite because it held that God appointed the king and that anyone who challenged the king's authority was also challenging God's authority. Anyone so audacious as to rebel against the edits of the ruling elite could not only be charged with treason, but the organized church could charge the rebel with heresy. America's founding fathers were well aware of how the ruling elite could pervert the church from its religious calling and use "religious" leaders to further the role of an oppressive government.

Americans, from the very beginning of the country, generally viewed with suspicion the role of government. The role of the federal government was especially viewed with suspicion, and no small amount of fear. As British colonies the thirteen original states had just seceded from a large, unresponsive, and oppressive central government in London, and they had no desire to replace one oppressive central government with another, especially one of their own creation. The first federal government for the United States was created under the Articles of Confederation. The Articles were signed on November 15, 1777. It is very important that all Americans understand the origin of the authority for this federal government and the one that followed it under the Constitution of 1789. When the Original Thirteen Colonies seceded from their union with Great Britain, they did so independently of each other. By the time the joint Declaration of Independence was signed some colonies had already seceded from Great Britain. The colony of Virginia passed in May 1776 a resolution declaring: "Resolved, that the union that has hitherto subsisted between Great Britain and the American Colonies is thereby totally dissolved, and that the inhabitants of *this* colony are discharged from any allegiance to the Crown of Great Britain."[1] (Emphasis added.) When the joint Declaration of Independence was signed on July 4, 1776, it clearly stated that all the colonies were free and independent states—note the use of plural "states." Great Britain signed the Treaty of Paris at the close of the Revolutionary War, thereby recognizing American independence. The treaty specifically recognized the independence of each colony individually—in other words, Great Britain did not grant independence to the United States of America *en masse* but to each former colony individually.

The Articles of Confederation that created the first federal government recognized this fact by boldly proclaiming that each member of the confederation came into the confederation as a free and independent state and retained its status as a free and independent state.[2] Specifically Article 2 of the Articles of Confederation stated:

1. James R. Kennedy and Walter D. Kennedy, *Was Jefferson Davis Right?* (Gretna, LA: Pelican Publishing Company, 1998), p. 258.

2. For a more detailed study of the Articles of Confederation's relationship to State's Rights see Kennedy and Kennedy, *Was Jefferson Davis Right?*, pp. 255-64.

"Each state retains its sovereignty, freedom, and independence..."
The Federal government, as originally established, received its
authority not from "we the people" directly but indirectly via each
sovereign state—the state served as the corporate representative
and ultimate protector of "we the people" at the local level. It
is "we the people" at the local level who make up the sovereign
community. The American political theory of State's Rights is the
only true means to protect the liberties of people within their local
communities from the oppressions of a federal government that
is disconnected from the people (the forgotten man). Without
State's Rights in its full vigor there is no way to protect the people
from an abusive Federal government that decides, for instance, to
declare that any statements made that homosexuality is forbidden
by God are to be punishable by the Federal government as a
hate crime. Where would "we the people" go if (when) immoral[3]
liberals/socialists who compose America's ruling elite declare our
religious views to be illegal? What protection is there in a written
constitution if there are no effective means to enforce its written
protections? Without State's Rights in its full vigor the Constitution
is useless! No! It is worst than useless, because too many Americans
will foolishly cling to the old and beloved document as if it possessed
magical powers to resurrect itself and one day "by and by" again
protect the reserved rights of "we the people!" That event will not
happen unless God's people make it happen!

Those anti-State's Rights, Federal supremacists, who over the
years have desired to enlarge the powers of the Federal government
in order to use those enlarged powers for personal gain,[4] have
successfully stigmatized the American political concept of State's
Rights (state sovereignty) by asserting that State's Rights was an
evil tool used to protect slavery, Jim Crow laws, white supremacy,

---

3. We believe that using the power of government to deprive the numerical
minority of their private property via taxation is nothing other than using
government as a cover or smoke screen behind which the elite can safely hide
while robbing the politically unconnected for the benefit of the politically
connected; therefore, yes we believe that socialism, nominal socialism, and
liberalism are immoral.

4. Political and economic gain.

and racial segregation. This is most unfortunate because it is impossible to maintain and protect the rights reserved to the people of the states under a written constitution if the people of the states do not have the means to prevent the more powerful federal government from encroaching upon their reserved rights. Slavery and racial segregation are no longer enforceable by law. The concepts of government-enforced slavery and racial segregation are repugnant to contemporary Christians. State's Rights in its proper perspective should be viewed as the right of "we the people" to control our local communities. Anyone today who attempts to deride State's Rights due to its historical association with slavery or racial segregation should be dismissed as one seeking Federal supremacy in order to force his will upon "we the people" of the sovereign community. In a phrase, "That was then, this is now!" Creating and sustaining a moral community now is our concern. It should also be remembered that the improper use of a moral principle does not negate the proper use of that principle. We are asserting the right of using State's Rights in its proper "American" context.

America's first government was based on the principle of local self-government and the desire to establish a non-threatening and non-intrusive federal government. The emphasis was on self-sufficiency, individual responsibility, and personal accountability. Most citizens would have some contact with the local government at the county/parish level, less contact with the state government, and virtually no contact with the federal government. This arrangement allowed for maximum freedom and minimal taxation, and it succored and encouraged strong families and vibrant local communities. The past one hundred and fifty years have seen a radical (and unconstitutional) increase in the power of the Federal government with a resultant decrease in morality, liberties, and property rights at the local level. For the past seventy-five years the traditional family and Christian morality, the bedrock of a healthy local community, have come under increasingly virulent attacks from America's ruling elite and their cronies. When governmental power is concentrated at the top, the forgotten man at the bottom is crushed. When government becomes the enemy of morality—what recourse is left for the minority who believe in moral values?

Minimal Government—Local Self-Government

The only acceptable government for those who truly believe in morality and who cherish individual liberty is minimal government—a government in which the federal government is ultimately subservient to "we the people" within our respective sovereign state. Local self-government will be responsible for protection of citizens' property rights, adjudicating local disputes, and supporting the local community's moral code. The manner in which such local "governmental" responsibilities will be carried out will vary within each sovereign community— that is, within each sovereign state. Some states may decide to experiment with private courts or privatize police protection services. Within the national confederation each sovereign state will be an experiment in local self-government. Successful experiments will be adopted by other states, and unsuccessful ones will be avoided. Unlike the current system in which all important issues are mandated and enforced from the federal level, the system of minimal government will allow "we the people" of the sovereign community acting through our corporate representative, the state, to decide what kind of society we want our children to inherit.

Minimal government means that the tax base that the current Federal government mandates will radically change. Currently Americans pay 40 to 60 percent of their income for taxes![5] Under a minimal government system the total taxing authority for all government (local, state, and Federal) will be capped at no more than 10 percent. Every workingman (the proverbial forgotten man) will take home, net pay, an amount equal to or almost equal to his gross pay (his pay before government expropriates its taxes from the money he earned by his labor).

Under this system, taxation above this level will be considered involuntary servitude—slavery! It's your money; you keep what you honestly earn. The only exception is the amount that is taxed (by whatever fashion your state elects to

5. James Ronald Kennedy, *Reclaiming Liberty* (Gretna, LA: Pelican Publishing Company, 2005), pp. 163-83.

use)[6] with your consent to maintain the necessary functions of government—local, state, and Federal.

6. Of all the ways to collect direct taxes, payroll deduction is the most dangerous to liberty—and must be avoided at all costs. It is better to have the taxpayer write one big check once a year—then the taxpayer gets to see just how much of his income property the government is stealing from him. Politicians, the ruling elite, find such a system very unattractive—all the more reason to adopt such a system.

8

Tax Consumers Versus Tax Payers

Principle Number 5: *Human government, regardless of its size or form, always divides people into those who benefit from government and those who pay for government.*

Democracy or Mobocracy?

America's founding fathers were so concerned about the possible excesses of popular democracy that some referred to democracy as "mobocracy." The excesses of the French Revolution (1790-99) remain as an example of the type of excesses the founding fathers sought to avoid when they established our American republic of republics.

The distinction between a representative republic of republics and a mass democracy was well understood at the founding of the United States. Most modern Americans have a vague understanding of what a democracy is but virtually no concept of the notion of a representative republic and even less knowledge of what features encompass a government described as a republic of republics.

Democracy, in its original meaning, simply meant "people rule." The ancient Greeks in Athens had a system of government in which the citizens would choose people to represent them in an assembly that was charged with making political decisions for Athens. This system works well if the population is relatively small and shares similar cultural and ethnic backgrounds. Both small size and similar background reduces (though certainly not eliminates) areas for conflict or competing group interests. In addition to these requirements those who exercised the privilege of voting had to meet certain qualifications to assure quality decisions. This is different from a town hall type of meeting in which anyone who is a member of the particular group is allowed to attend and participate in the discussion, and then the group makes the final decision. A town hall type of government is mass democracy in action and can degenerate into what the founding fathers termed "mobocracy."

Mobocracy occurs when competing group interests become a part of the debate over government action, and the larger "mob" controls the outcome of any question, thus assuring its interests are served at the expense of other groups.

The founding fathers avoided the use of the term "democracy" and instead used the term "republic." In the Constitution they even required the Federal government to assure that every state had a republican form of government in order to become a member of the Union.[1] Each state is required to be a republic, and the individual states are members of a republic; therefore, the term "republic [singular] of republics [plural]." Each state is free, independent, and sovereign. Each state has original sovereignty and acts as the corporate representative of the sovereign community within that state. The sovereign state (a republic) sends representatives to the Federal Congress to represent the will of the sovereign community within the state. The power or authority of the Federal government (as originally established)[2] was limited by a written constitution that specified what authority the sovereign states agreed to delegate (not surrender) to the Federal government. With the exception of Article I, Section 10, the entire original Federal Constitution was designed to document what powers the states voluntarily agreed to allow the Federal government to exercise—*conditionally*. The controlling condition set by the sovereign states was that the delegated powers be used "pursuant to the Constitution." Acts by the Federal government outside of those specifically authorized by the contract agreed to by the sovereign states (the Constitution) would be unconstitutional and therefore null and void, having no authority over a sovereign state. That was the founding fathers' original intention, but that, as we all know, is a far cry from what exists today.

The Fear of King Numbers
Many Americans are shocked to learn of the founding fathers'

---

1. Article IV, Section 4, United States Constitution.
2. For a detailed account of how the original intentions of the founding fathers was usurped and perverted to the current regime of Federal supremacy, see James Ronald Kennedy and Walter Donald Kennedy, *The South Was Right!* & *Why Not Freedom!* (Gretna, LA: Pelican Publishing Company, 1994 & 1995).

fear of mass democracy. America's education establishment has done a great disservice by "educating" (or more aptly put, indoctrinating) Americans about the wonders of America's democracy. James Madison, known as the Father of the Constitution, made it very clear during the debates on whether or not to ratify the new constitution that he did not favor any system that might lead to mass democracy. *The Federalist No. 10* records Madison's words:

> [A] pure democracy...A common passion or interest will, in almost every case, be felt by a majority of the whole... [Such governments] have ever been found incompatible with personal security or the rights of property... [T]his species of government, have erroneously supposed that by reducing mankind to a perfect equality in their political rights, they would, at the same time be perfectly equalized and assimilated in their possessions, their opinions, and their passions.[3]

Note Madison's warning that the "majority of the whole" would use the force of government to oppress "property rights." He also warned that when people operate in a group (mob or government) their emotions and passions tend toward the lowest common denominator of the group. It should be of no surprise that mass democracies always degenerate into governments that actively seek to "redistribute" wealth in order to assure that no one has "too much" and that everyone in society has "their fair share." Parallel to the urge to equalize wealth, mass democracies also attempt to enforce the lowest form of social morality, regardless of how far removed it is from biblical views.

In a mass democracy the majority of the voters demand not only social equality but equality of results. The opinions, passions, and biases of the masses are constantly provoked by politicians seeking votes from the mass of society by lamenting how unfairly society treats some and how unfair it is that others have more than they actually need. Such politicians gain the votes of the masses by promising government action to "redistribute" wealth from those with too much to those who have less. Of course, as we have

3. James Madison, as cited in, Kennedy and Kennedy, *Why Not Freedom!*, p. 181.

already noted, government has no resources of its own; therefore, in order to give something to the aroused masses, politicians enact oppressive taxes on the productive element of society to fund their political debt to the masses. Madison knew that a mass democracy would degenerate into a system in which clever politicians would use the power of government to expropriate wealth from those who have no connections with the ruling elite, and then use portions of the expropriated wealth to pay off those voting blocs that were responsible for electing the members of the ruling elite in the first place. In short, democracy eventually becomes a vote-buying scheme in which the ruling elite use the wealth of those with no political power to pay for the votes they purchased in the last election. Yes, the politicians purchased their votes by giving their voters an IOU during the previous election campaign—a promise to redistribute wealth via government programs to benefit the politicians' voting bloc. All this is done in a democracy via majority vote—all perfectly legal within the democratic framework.

Democratic governments may not start out that way, but as John C. Calhoun noted, eventually the numerical majority (King Numbers) realizes that it can legally consume as much of the wealth of the numerical minority as it desires—majority rule! Of course, in a republic of republics it is impossible for the federal government to expropriate the wealth of the numerical minority because the sovereign state can interpose its sovereign authority between an abusive federal government and the citizens of that state. Unfortunately, Americans no longer live in a constitutionally limited republic of republics.

Tipping Point in Modern America

Most democracies begin with a population in which there are more productive adult citizens than nonproductive adult citizens. Think of society as a balance scale in which the number (weight) of productive citizens greatly exceeds the number (weight) of nonproductive citizens. In such a state of affairs it seems almost immoral not to allow politicians to "help" the downtrodden who need "not a handout, but a hand up!" But as more and more government handouts become available something very predictable occurs—the mass of voters who are in need does *not* decrease, but rather it actually increases! A basic axiom of free-market economics is that "the more government subsidizes something, the more of that thing it produces!" Common sense would tell a business person or a laborer that if he does something and the net cost to him is more each time he does it, then he should stop doing that particular thing. But politicians do not work by such common sense dictates. In the world of the ruling elite, they do not have to bear the cost of programs they enact; plus such programs increase their potential to receive the votes from those who benefit from government programs; then it makes perfect sense not only to continue such costly programs, but to increase them to cover as many voters as possible. This is why the Federal Congress has a 90-plus percent incumbency rate—the ruling elite use taxpayers' money to "legally" buy their way back into office.

The presidential election of 2008 represented the tipping point for American democracy—the point at which those who benefit from government programs can outvote those who pay for government programs—the taxpayer has become America's forgotten man. Some economists have been trying to warn Americans about the crisis that big government is creating.

> The sequence is always the same, High-tax, big-spending policies force the economy to lose momentum. Then growth in government spending outstrips revenues. Fiscal and trade deficits soar. Public debt, excessive taxation and unemployment follow. The central bank tries to solve the problem by printing money...The system stagnates.[4]

The problem as identified by Calhoun in the 1840s is that eventually those who demand big government spending programs outvote those who have to pay for such programs. Those who benefit from government programs are the tax consumers. Tax consumers are individuals and groups such as: politicians, bureaucrats, special interest groups, social welfare recipients, corporate welfare recipients, and social activists such as gay rights

---

4. Adam Lerrick, "Obama and the Tax-Tipping Point," *The Wall Street Journal*, Wednesday, October 22, 2008, p. A17.

groups, environmental groups, feminists, secular humanists, liberals, nominal socialists, and socialists.

Notice how democracy ultimately degenerates into a system that divides citizens against each other—those who pay and those who benefit. Liberals are quick to claim that those who advocate Christian morality are intolerant and "divisive." Yet the truth is that it is liberals who divide American citizens into warring camps. As Calhoun warned more than 150 years ago, there is no limit to the exploitation that will occur once the numerical majority learns it can use the force of government to compel the numerical minority to surrender its wealth for "socially good" purposes. As bad (immoral) as the theft of wealth from productive citizens may be, there is an even greater immorality now being forced upon the moral numerical minority. The greatest immorality is that liberals and secular humanists can now "legalize" oppressive government intrusions and use the force of government to eliminate politically incorrect political views. How long will it be before those who preach sermons that are not politically correct will be subject to charges of hate crimes and prosecuted by the Federal Office for Civil Rights? Liberals and secular humanists can now use monies expropriated from the moral numerical minority to finance programs that encourage immorality. The current system of American government has reached the moral tipping point as well as the tax tipping point!

9

Dictators in a Democracy

Principle Number 6: *Democratic government always favors leaders (politicians) who are power hungry, aggressive, egotistical, and who are willing to compromise on principle for the sake of gaining or maintaining power.*

Electing the Best Man

At every election cycle Americans take time out of their busy life to go the voting polls to cast their ballot in the hope of electing the best person for the job. The sad truth is that the best man is never on the ballot! Invariably, the productive citizen goes into the voting booth and is forced to select between the lesser of two evils. Many of the founding fathers envisioned a country in which gentlemen would be compelled by their sense of civic duty to dedicate a portion of their time to public service and then return to manage their private affairs. But the passions of greed and envy will always drive some people to seek political office, not to serve others but to selfishly enrich themselves and those close to them—although they will certainly package their campaign for elected office in a manner that will cause voters to believe that public service is the candidate's only motive for seeking elected office. Christians more than any other group of people should understand why this is a constant problem. Sin and its corrosive consequences are inborn with all humanity. The founding fathers of this nation understood this fact, but unfortunately many modern Americans either have forgotten this fact or openly deny that sin is a problem. The problem with democracies is that the contest to elect individuals to public office is won by the politician who can persuade the largest number of voters that those who vote for him will receive more benefits than they will if they vote for any of his opponents. Political promises are made just as easily as they are broken. Indeed, most political promises are made with the expectation that only part if any of the promises will be kept by the politician.

Political promises are not new to American politics. During the days of Reconstruction (1867-77), Northern-dominated carpetbag and scalawag politicians promised newly enfranchised former slaves "forty acres and a mule" if they would vote for them. This promise, among many subsequent promises, was never kept. But politicians keep making promises; some they deliver on, most they don't, but election after election the process is repeated. For the past sixty years the voters of New York City have been promised a new Second Avenue subway.[1] On several occasions they have even voted in favor of taxes or bonds to pay for the new subway. But somehow even though money has been appropriated, the new subway has not been built! This may be an extreme but not an unusual example of the sea of political lies in which American freedom is slowly drowning. In modern America, politics is the art of broken promises.

Can a Moral Person Win an Election?

Moral people do not tell lies. Moral people keep their promises unless providentially hindered. But in order to raise sufficient money to run a winning political campaign in contemporary America a candidate must do three essentially immoral things: (1) promise to take money away from those who honestly earned it (theft even if it is blessed and sanctified by a majority vote) and give it to those who have no legal right to it; (2) make promises that most likely will not be kept; and (3) make promises—either actual or implied—to grant certain favors to individuals and groups who provide the financing for the winning campaign. This raises the question: "Can a moral person be elected to political office?"

Christians understand from their knowledge of the inherent nature of man that man will always have the tendency to feel more keenly what affects him personally than what affects others. They also know that there are always certain small numbers of men who feel this passion more than others and/or have weaker motives to control or discipline this selfish passion. The truth is that in all societies there have always been and always will be certain men

---

1. Gregory Bresiger, "Subway Hijinks," http://mises.org/story/3324 (accessed 5/18/2009).

who not only covet the property of others but who will engage in immoral stratagems to gain other people's wealth or property. Acting as individuals these people participate in both petty and major crimes against the person and property of those productive members of society who have honestly earned their wealth. This can be dangerous and generally does not pay off too well for the criminal. But when these individuals decide to engage in politics, the danger is removed. Politicians legalize theft by calling it taxation, and the payoff for the ruling elite and those close to the ruling elite is enormous.

Successful leaders in a democratic society tend to be those who are not hindered by strong moral principles. Such individuals can easily rationalize making promises they know they will not keep, breaking promises they thought they were going to keep, or hedging on principles to further their own interests. To fill this role candidates must have certain personality traits. They must be egotistical. They have to have an inflated self-image and an enlarged sense of self-importance. In addition they must be aggressive. As a rule there are very few easygoing, gentlemanly types in the chambers of any democratic legislature. The only way to be a successful politician in a mass democracy is to be a person with little or no moral inhibitions against expropriating other peoples' property. Only an unprincipled person can successfully piece together majority votes in a legislature made up of numerous conflicting special interest groups. Only the most efficient demigods can bring together and hold together voters who have nothing in common except a desire to use the power of government to extort money from the productive element of society. By its very nature, democratic government attracts individuals who would not do well in the competition of a free market where in order to succeed they must consistently provide the consumer with the best product at the lowest possible price. These individuals know that there are only two ways for them to acquire wealth: (1) by being a productive member of society and providing goods and services to consumers at a quality and price the consumer will accept, or (2) by exploiting the productive members of society via criminal or governmental acts.

"Social conservatives" were shocked by the public exposure of "conservative" Republican elected officials who had engaged in immoral acts subsequent to having been elected even though these politicians ran their campaigns claiming to be "moral, social, or family values" conservatives. This should come as no surprise in light of the type of people who are naturally selected in America's modern mass democracy. Once elected, even individuals who are initially dedicated to moral or conservative values become mesmerized by or intoxicated with the perks and privileges of power. Most successful politicians have what some psychologists call a Type A personality. People with this type of personality are aggressive, driven, success oriented, impatient, and highly competitive. Very few, if any, politicians can succeed in America's current political system if they do not have these traits. Therefore it is reasonable to assume that mass democracies tend to select such individuals as leaders. When government gives power to such people it should not be surprising that they tend to abuse their power. Before we answer the question regarding whether a moral person can be elected, let us take a look at our founding fathers' attitude toward the potential of leaders to abuse their offices for personal gain.

Men or Angels to Rule Over Us?

Both Thomas Jefferson and James Madison were very skeptical of man's ability to justly rule over his fellows. Madison declared, "If men were angels no government would be necessary....if angels were to govern men, no controls on government would be necessary."[2] Jefferson joined in by observing, "...[I]t is said that man cannot be trusted with the government of himself. Can he, then, be trusted with the government of others? Or have we found angels in the forms of kings to govern him?"[3] Jefferson was especially concerned about the possible abuse of governmental power by those elected to serve the public. He even went so far as to acknowledge the fact that if the public became inattentive to the excesses of elected leaders and failed to timely correct or remove corrupt officials, the temptation to engage in abuse of powers would reach all elected officials:

2. James Madison, as cited in, James R. Kennedy and Walter D. Kennedy, *Was Jefferson Davis Right?* (Gretna, LA: Pelican Publishing Company, 1998), p. 223.
3. Thomas Jefferson, as quoted in, Kennedy and Kennedy, *Was Jefferson Davis Right?* p. 225.

Cherish therefore the spirit of our people...If once they become inattentive to the public affairs, you and I, and Congress, and Assemblies, judges and governors, shall all become as wolves.[4]

Thomas Jefferson and James Madison were both aware of the tendency of even good men once elected to abuse their power. Again, we must point out that as Christians we understand that the sinful nature of even "good" men prevents mankind from establishing a utopian society. As Jefferson and Madison pointed out, if men were angels no government would be needed. But we are sinful creatures; therefore, we need government, but we also need a government that we can control. As Jefferson pointed out, if governments are not controlled, the men who control government will "become as wolves."

This fact was borne out by a little-known incident that occurred at the close of President George Washington's second term in office. Of all people in American history no one better demonstrates the principle of public service than George Washington. At the close of the Revolutionary War the ill-supplied Continental army was running out of patience with the Congress's failure to supply and pay the army. The promised appropriations to pay the troops and officers had again failed to materialize. During a meeting of his staff a disgruntled and angered officer suggested that General Washington lead the army to Philadelphia, disband Congress, and take over the government. It could have been done, because General Washington commanded the largest army in the country and also commanded the respect of the majority of Americans. But General Washington refused. For this he is known as the American Cincinnatus.

But even George Washington could not resist the temptation to use his office to turn a small profit. At the close of his second term as president there was a great debate between those, led by Alexander Hamilton, who wanted to enlarge the Federal government by establishing a national bank, and those, led by Thomas Jefferson,

---

4. Thomas Jefferson, as cited in, William J. Quirk and R. Randall Bridwell, *Judicial Dictatorship* (New Brunswich, NJ: Transaction Publishers, 1995), p. 1.

who declared that the Constitution gave no specific authority for such an act. President Washington made a deal with certain elected officials that in exchange for his support for the Federal bank bill they would support a bill to move the national capital to an area between Virginia and Maryland (subsequently to be known as Washington, D.C.). It just so happened that George Washington owned land in that exact same area and stood to benefit from such an agreement. The implied powers used to justify the establishment of a Federal bank became a key weapon for those seeking to enlarge the powers of the Federal government. Remember that the Constitution nowhere allows such "powers" for the Federal government. It is the Hamiltonian constitutional theory of "implied powers" that the Supreme Court has used to assert Federal supremacy ever since. The Federal Supreme Court quickly adopted the Hamiltonian doctrine of implied powers and used it to remove the limitations placed upon the acts of the Federal government by the Constitution. This was the beginning of the end for State's Rights.

The answer to the question of whether or not a moral person can win election in America today is—No. Even if he gained victory, which is highly unlikely today, it would take a most unusual person possessed with almost superhuman personality traits to resist the temptations of power inherent in America's current political system. "But where does that leave us?" you may ask. *The way to elect moral people to office is to change the current system by removing the possibility of perks and power.* How to do that is discussed in a later section of this book.

10

Creating Wealth That Benefits Everyone

Principle Number 7: *The free market is the only way that social wealth is created or increased.*

Where Does Wealth Come From?

God's instruction to man "Six days shalt thou labor" and the eighth commandment "Thou shall not steal" demonstrate that man is to be productive. This God-ordained activity in a free society produces what we may refer to as "wealth." When this activity is multiplied thousands of times as each individual in society "earns his bread by the sweat of his brow," the result is a viable economic system. From the beginning of time it was man's economic activity that created wealth; so man does not need government to "jump start" the economy. Yet, every time the economy experiences a downturn, recession, or depression, there arises a cry for government to do something to get the economy "going" again. This plea for economic salvation comes first from those who love big government. Then they are joined by many well-meaning but economically confused people. Liberals (nominal socialists) and left-wing extremists (Marxists or neo-Marxists) who by their principles naturally hate the free market (capitalist) system now control the mass media and the system of public higher education. They have done a great job of confusing people about basic economic principles by propagating their erroneous anti-free market ideology. But in all their laments about how unfair the free-market system is, in all of their confusing and misguided statistics about the number of people held in poverty by the free-market system, and their feigned[1]

---

1. "Feigned" is used because they are never heard complaining about those close to them making too much money. Vile and vulgar Hollywood elite and of course professional sports heroes are never their target—only those who gain their wealth honestly from the free market.

distress about too much wealth being held by a few; in all of this they never stop to explain where wealth comes from in the first place. Any common criminal can steal a car and give it to a friend, but it takes something very special to create the car in the first place. That special something necessary to create a car (an example of things that compose social wealth) is called freedom—free men and women voluntarily cooperating with each other using their own resources and ability to create wealth that will benefit all of those lucky enough (blessed by God) to live in such a society! Wealth comes from free people working for their own enlightened self-interest. But remember, in the free market an individual's self-interest (his God-given desire to gain wealth) cannot be fulfilled if the individual does not produce something that others will *voluntarily* exchange their money in order to obtain. In the free market, wealth is created by the voluntary interaction of people, and the consumer is king. If the consumer is not pleased with a product, then the producer (this includes those who labor for a wage) suffers loss or goes out of business (or loses his job). The free market rewards productive endeavors and chastises nonproductive endeavors, but this is different in the world of politics. In the world of government the politician is king, and "we the people" are compelled by the force of government to submit. Net increase in social wealth is never the ultimate outcome. Even though "we the people" see more and more of our money being taken by government, we have no option but to submit—because the politician is king! Yes, the politicians, our ruling elite, are the masters in our current system of centralized federalism. Remember, this is not the system our founding fathers gave us; it is the system politicians have perverted and now use against the forgotten man for the benefit of the ruling elite.

Other Peoples' Money—What Politicians Let People See

Anytime the cry goes up for government intervention into the free market—which includes taxation, because it limits people's ability to fund things they need—anytime the force of government is used to compel (force) people to do something that they do not want to do, such as funding partial birth abortions or advancing the homosexual agenda, there will be a net loss of social wealth and a net gain of political wealth. Political wealth is created by government when politicians use their elected office to gain the perks and prestige of power and economic advantages for themselves and those close to them. Those "close to" politicians include those who contribute large amounts of money (directly and indirectly) to the election/re-election of the politicians, special interest groups that provide large voting blocs to assure the politicians' election/re-election, and at the national level those associated with the large Wall Street financial institutions and corporations that depend on the Federal Reserve for their financial success. Once elected to office, politicians reward those who put them in office by redistributing increasingly larger amounts of OPM (other peoples' money).

Politicians love to spend and give away OPM. Spending OPM helps politicians to cement their relations with the voters. Politicians are quick to offer their constituents "free" programs and projects. They never remind them that the dollars spent were taken away from other taxpayers who are now demanding that their representatives take away some of other people's property, via taxation, to fund similar "free" projects and programs for them. As the American political con game of "tax each other to get free government projects and programs" has continued to grow, it has become apparent that some people (or groups) are net gainers—they receive more from government than they pay in taxes—while others are net losers—they pay more in taxes than they receive in government benefits. Once a country reaches the tipping point—the point where the net gainers, those receiving more government benefits, outvote the net losers, those receiving fewer government benefits; the smaller group of taxpayers (the numerical minority) have become the captives of the numerical majority. The numerical majority will use the police and taxing power of government to extract (steal) more and more wealth from the numerical minority. Not only have the taxpayers become the tax slaves of the tax consumers, but the eighth commandment against stealing has now been routinely trampled on by the government "of the people, by the people, and for the people"!

OPM—What People Do Not See

Politicians love to brag about all the benefits provided by government: "free" health care, "free" food for the needy, "free" education for those who could not otherwise afford it, "free" roads and infrastructure, etc. This is what they want the public to see, but what about the things the public never sees? Things such as positive and productive economic developments that would have occurred had "we the people" been allowed to keep our money and invest or spend our money for things that would have been in the best interest of the people who had legitimately earned the money. It is not possible for people to see the activity that would have occurred had it not been for government forcefully taking away people's money. Activity such as job creation and an increase in social wealth cannot be seen because government prevents if from ever occurring. People cannot see or count something that never happens—and this works to the benefit of all politicians. People see new bridges and roads, but they never see what economists call the opportunity costs of those government activities—the lost opportunity of "we the people" to do something positive and productive with our money. Economists[2] refer to this situation as the broken window fallacy.

If a mischievous boy goes around town with his slingshot breaking windows, are his acts good for the economy? Some people would answer in the affirmative. Some people believe that because the supply business has to sell windows to replace those broken, and contractors have to pay workers to replace the broken windows, then the economy has been improved or stimulated. Thus, economic activity has been greatly increased as a result of the boy's mischievous acts—indeed, according to this logic the boy should receive a reward for his efforts to stimulate the economy! This is the essence of the dangers of not being able to readily see those things that did not occur due to people being forced, by the mischievous boy, to spend their money on things that would not have been their first choice.

People are deceived because they make an economic assessment by taking into account only what they see—a sharp increase in business activity (for window suppliers and window replacement

---

2. Not all economists would agree with this concept. Those who favor government intervention, the nominal and actual socialists, would favor taking money away from the productive and using it to "stimulate" the economy while achieving social justice by redistributing wealth away from those who earned it and giving it to those who have no legitimate claim on other people's money. Warning people about this "broken window" fallacy is an integral part of Austrian economic thought.

laborers), but they do not consider what is not seen. What the people do not see is the increase in social wealth that was not allowed to occur. Broken windows were replaced, but overall values of the affected buildings did not increase. Economists would say that there was no net increase in social capital. The property did not lose value, but neither did it gain productive value. Nothing was added to the property that made it more productive or better able to provide goods and services at a cost or quality better than that which existed before the expenditures were made to replace the broken windows. At best, social wealth[3] merely stayed the same. But this too is an incomplete assessment.

The real loss occurred due to the fact that business people were forced to take money away from ongoing and potentially profitable business opportunities and use that money to pay for the replacement of destroyed current assets. What people don't see are all the sustainable jobs that would have been created or the increase in quality or decrease in price of commodities that would have been offered to the consumer had the business person been allowed to use his money to improve or expand his business. Increased economic activity or economic stimulus via broken windows is an obvious fallacy once people stop, pull back, and review everything that happens and consider things that were not allowed to happen. Nothing socially positive or productive occurs when an external force (the mischievous boy in this example) compels people to spend their money on something for which they would not have voluntarily elected to spend their limited resources. Now, replace the mischievous boy with politicians using the police and taxing power of government, and you will see that the outcome is the same—social wealth or the potential to increase social wealth is destroyed! The only difference between the mischievous boy and politicians is that the acts of the mischievous boy are physically limited (there is a limited amount of damage he can do to society as a whole) and are illegal, but the acts of politicians are unlimited and affect all of society, plus the acts of the politicians are considered "legal" as a result of gaining a majority vote in the previous election.

---

3. Social wealth is the total value of all privately held assets in society.

Taxing individuals and businesses in order to give the ruling elite OPM to spend on "free" government programs and projects is an example of the broken window fallacy gone wild! Politicians do not create or add to social wealth. Government at best impedes the growth of social wealth, and at worst it actually destroys social wealth.

The Free Market and the Creation of Social Wealth

In the post-Eden world there are only two ways in which man can obtain wealth: (1) by being productive, or (2) by being parasitic. The productive way is what most people would refer to as the morally correct way to acquire wealth.[4] Productive people offer goods or services to consumers who then voluntarily decide whether the benefit gained from the offered goods or services is of greater value than the money spent to obtain them. Note two very important facts about transactions in the free market: (1) everything is done through voluntary agreement between the parties, and (2) at the conclusion of the transaction both parties have gained! Force is not an element of the transaction, and both parties gain something of value. Not only does the free market increase social wealth, it also encourages (in fact, it requires) mutual respect and cooperation between people who may not even like each other! The parasitic way of gaining wealth is far different. By the very nature of a parasite there must be a host to supply sustenance to the parasite. A leach gains its sustenance from the blood of the host. Note that the host does not voluntarily accept the presence of the parasite, but circumstances force the host to accept the parasite. In the human setting social parasites are those who live by depriving or extorting the property of the productive members of society. A criminal is an example of a social parasite. His lack of morals allows him to follow a criminal lifestyle. His possession of superior cunning and greater physical power allows him to pursue his chosen lifestyle—all to the detriment of the productive class—causing a general decrease in

---

4. The term "wealth" is used to denote material goods that improve man's condition. A primitive man who creates a stone tool is wealthy as compared to his fellow who as of yet does not have such a tool. The more tools creative men produce and hold as private property, the wealthier society in general becomes. As society becomes wealthier, man's living conditions improve.

actual and potential social wealth. Pursuing a parasitic lifestyle as a criminal is usually risk laden—at some point the productive class may decide to seize the criminal and apply appropriate punishment. A safer and more socially acceptable form of parasitic living is to gain one's sustenance from society via the administration of social governance (politics) and/or social or corporate welfare. Politicians are absolutely indispensible for the dispersion of OPM to fund both social and corporate welfare. The unholy trinity of politicians, corporate welfare recipients, and social welfare recipients compose the most dangerous threat to the free market and individual liberty in America's mass democracy. The individual and collective actions of this "unholy trinity" are the driving forces behind the downward spiral of morality in the past one hundred years of American history.

The free market creates wealth, but the ruling elite seize portions of other people's wealth via taxation and redistribute other people's wealth to those closely associated with the ruling elite. Politicians destroy wealth, government impedes the development of new wealth, and parasites consume the hopes and dreams of the moral, law-abiding, productive element of society. Socialism, regardless of the in-vogue name it goes by, has always been a tool used by the immoral and unproductive to oppress the moral and productive members of society. Modern-day Christians should remember the warning issued by the great evangelical Baptist minister Charles Spurgeon: "I would not have you exchange the gold of individual Christianity for the base metal of Christian Socialism."[5]

---

5. "Spurgeon On Socialism," Joel McDurman, www.americanvision.org/article/ spurgeon-on-socialism, (accessed March 6, 2009).

11

Statesmen or Politicians?

Principle Number 8: *Elected leaders in a political system of minimum government will be universally acknowledged as statesmen.*

The Death of Outrage

Opinion surveys have consistently demonstrated that the American people hold politicians in contempt. Why would Americans have such a low opinion of people who win democratic popularity contests known as elections? The sad but simple fact is that Americans have come to expect (and receive) the worst from the people they elect. If a popular president is caught, in the White House, having an illicit sexual affair with a young girl, there is no moral outrage; if a male member of Congress is caught texting male employees seeking sexual favors, there is no moral outrage; if a male member of Congress is caught soliciting homosexual favors in a public restroom, there is no moral outrage; if a conservative "family values" member of the Senate is caught paying harlots for sexual services, there is no moral outrage; the list could go on almost indefinitely! And if the list did continue until it included all the immoral acts[1] of "our" elected leaders, it would include only those outrageous acts in which they have been caught! Only God knows the full extent of their immorality—enabled by the perks and powers "we the people" granted them when they were elected to carry out public duties.

No doubt many moral Americans were shocked when these and

---

1. Political immoral acts are not just acts of sexual immorality; they include all acts of politicians that further their personal agenda and enrich those close to them. Such political acts are immoral because the benefits derived by the ruling elite and those close to the ruling elite are paid for by extracting, under the implied threat of force, private property and liberty from productive citizens.

other events were disclosed. Even though many moral Americans were shocked, the vast majority of Americans merely shrugged and looked the other way. The point is that events such as those listed have occurred so often the American public has become desensitized to the ruling elite's immoral acts. Americans have come to accept immoral and outrageous acts of elected politicians, and as a result such acts have become *de facto* acceptable. There is an old saying, "Silence gives consent." Based on that standard the American people, by their failure to demonstrate moral outrage and drive errant politicians out of office, have become party to the immorality of the ruling elite. The ruling elite have engaged in outrageous immoral acts, and "we the people" by our silence have merely stood by and held their coats. Or so it would appear.

There are large numbers of moral people who were and are outraged by such acts of "our" elected leaders. But the failure to rise up and remove the offenders may not be due to moral apathy but to learned indifference. "Learned indifference" is a psychological term that was developed to describe the condition that arises when a person finds himself in a position that he knows will result in personal pain or harm, but from experience he has learned that there is absolutely nothing he can do about the approaching pain or harm—all that is left for him to do is to remain docile and await the inevitable consequence. Psychologists studied this phenomenon by taking a test animal and putting the poor creature in a box with a metal floor. They would then ring a bell, wait a few seconds, and then apply a nonlethal but painful electrical current to the metal floor. After a few ringing bells followed by electrical shocks the animal learned to anticipate the coming pain and would scurry about in the box attempting to find a place of safety. After a number of additional shocks the animal learned that there was no place to hide from the coming pain. Once the animal learned that there was nothing it could do to avoid the pain, the poor animal would merely stand quivering, waiting for the coming shock as soon as it heard the ringing of the bell. The animal had learned to be indifferent about the coming pain that was about to be delivered. Notice that even though the animal was no longer trying to prevent or avoid the pain—it felt the pain nonetheless. And so it is with "we the people." Under the current political system there is very little "we the people" can do to correct the inherently immoral nature of the very system that produces the immoral politicians who rule over us.

What Is a Statesman?

The word "statesman" is little used in modern America. More often when it is used it is in fact misused. When the liberal media use the term they mean a successful politician, one who has learned the technique of using OPM (other people's money) to buy incumbency and assure that he and those close to him reap the benefits available to those who control government—the ruling elite.

This definition is better applied to politicians. Statesmen are the exact opposite of politicians. Politicians tend toward immorality in government and life, whereas statesmen tend toward morality in government and their personal life. Because both statesmen and politicians are fallen creatures (as are all people), neither should be viewed as being immune from immoral acts. Even the best statesmen in American history had their failings, faults, and shortcomings. The difference is that the likelihood or probability of the *politician* abusing his powers to benefit himself, his friends, and those close to government is much higher than that of the *statesman*. The negative impact of immoral political acts on society is demonstrated by the fact that a political act is a sum-zero gain—one person or group gains at the expense of another, usually less powerful, person or group. While political acts may grant some generalized social benefit to "we the people," the net impact is that the ruling elite (and those close to the ruling elite) gain, while "we the people" lose. The loss suffered by "we the people" appears in the form of private property taken by the government via levy (taxation) and confiscation (eminent domain); a decrease in the purchasing power of money (inflation); or restrictions on liberty by the passage of laws, rules, and regulations (legislation); and the issuance of court orders (judicial decisions and edicts). Statesmen dedicate themselves to improving society primarily by assuring that government restricts its activities to those few, specific, and limited areas in which society has consented to allow government activities. Politicians on the other hand seek to increase the size and scope of government, because the bigger the government the larger their power—the larger their political power the greater the opportunity for self-aggrandizement and enrichment.

The measure of good leaders (statesmen) in a free society is: (1) they do not want or seek the position of political power, but at the behest of the community are willing to temporarily fill the political role, and (2) upon completion of their tenure in office neither they nor their family, nor anyone politically associated with them, has any more wealth than when the leaders assumed office (in other words, the statesmen did not use their public office to enrich themselves or those close to them).

The founding fathers intended public service to be an act of duty in which a respected member of the local community was elected to office. It was assumed that this respected citizen would not use the elected office as his primary means of support. The respected citizen would serve, but the very act of service would be a personal sacrifice—he would take time out of his personal business affairs in order to temporarily provide public service. Because the respected citizen was an honest and moral person, he knew that the time spent doing the public's business would result in a net loss for his private business. Public office was not a prize or honor to be sought, but a duty and service to be accepted.

"We the people" should always be suspicious of those who "want" to hold public office. Why would someone spend more money to gain a public office than he will receive in pay while holding that office? The answer is sad but true, and it shows just how smart the founding fathers were. Politicians spend more money to gain a public position than that position pays because they know that the perks, prestige, and power of public office in America's current democracy can be readily transferred into financial gain for the officeholder and those close to the officeholder. The perks, prestige, and power of public office will repay the politician far in excess of the amount it costs to run a successful political campaign.

The second measure of a statesman is that when he completes his tenure in office he leaves that office and returns to tend his private business affairs. Statesmen do not establish a ruling elite. Statesmen do not seek incumbency; they desire to return to their own private business affairs. The argument is made by some that it is good to re-elect people to office because the longer they are in office the better they know the system. This is exactly why we should not re-elect people to office. Remember that the vast majority of the things that government does today could be done better by the free market—if they need to be done at all! When did anyone hear of a longtime politician leaving office with less wealth than he had when he came to office? When did anyone hear of a longtime politician leaving office, and none of the business interests, social special interest groups, or his friends and relatives who had contributed large amounts to his election had not gained something of value as a result of the actions of the officeholder? And most important, who paid for the values and benefits gained as a result of political decision-making?

Can We Have a Political System That Encourages Rule by Statesmen?

"We the people" are now faced with three difficult questions: (1) Can a political system be designed that will encourage rule by statesmen and discourage rule by politicians? (2) How can "we the people" avoid establishing a "ruling elite?" and (3) How can "we the people" establish a system to check the natural tendency of those who control the reins of governmental power to abuse those powers? Any country boy knows that honey attracts flies, and if the honey is removed the flies will leave. In government, OPM is the honey and politicians are the flies. Big government has the power to accumulate massive amounts of OPM and the mechanism to legally extort even more as needed. This is one of the main reasons the founding fathers established a system of limited federalism—they did not want an all-powerful central government that would tax the forgotten man for the benefit of the ruling elite. Thomas Jefferson best described the concept of limited federalism when he declared the cost of the federal government would be almost unfelt by the average citizen. Jefferson explained his view of the federal government as a "...frugal government...[that does] not take from the mouth of labor the bread it has earned."[2] A frugal government needs very little, and therefore has very little OPM. Therefore it is very unattractive to those individuals whose ethical values would not prevent them from using government to extort money from others for their personal benefit. When faced by such circumstances in a constitutionally limited governmental system, those tending toward a parasitic lifestyle must either: (1) seek to sustain themselves by becoming productive members of society; (2) transfer their energy from legal looting via government to outright

2. Thomas Jefferson's first inaugural address, as cited in, James R. Kennedy and Donald W. Kennedy, *Was Jefferson Davis Right?* (Gretna, LA: Pelican Publishing Company, 1998), pp. 229-30.

illegal looting via criminal activity; or (3) gain public office and seek to enlarge the power of limited government in order to use the enlarged powers for their benefit and the benefit of those who support their unconstitutional efforts.

The wonderful thing about minimal government is that the small amount of OPM represents (relative to today's big government) a minimal opportunity for an elected leader to abuse his power. This means that those who are not a part of the political process have little to fear from government led by statesmen. Limited OPM also limits the temptation to develop a ruling elite, because there is no "payoff" to remaining in a political office—indeed the payoff comes when the statesman leaves public service and returns to manage his own business. The reason the founding fathers wanted successful people to hold public office was because they knew that to assure the continued success of their private business affairs the statesmen needed to return to their private business as soon as possible. Staying in power for these elected public servants was a true opportunity cost that they willingly bore in order to temporarily serve the public good. The motive for a statesman is to serve the public good even though it costs him personally, while the motive for a politician is to gain power to serve himself and those closely associated with the ruling elite. Minimal government encourages statesmanship, while big government encourages political parasitism.

Moral people have been taught from childhood that "the love of money is the root of all evil" (1 Timothy 6:10). OPM in government is the attractive nuisance that lures parasitic people into government service. Many may enter politics thinking that they will use their office to "do good" or "help the unfortunate," neither of which is a legitimate role of government—that role belongs to the moral people within each community as part of their God-ordained requirement as moral people. Unfortunately and predictably, the end result of human nature is that because it costs so much to win an election, the person who wins an election in America's current political system must find a way to repay those who financed his election. That way is through the dispensing of OPM either directly via social or corporate welfare; or indirectly via schemes such as the letting of government contracts and the resulting cost overruns, or contracts made at full price but delivered with very poor quality—no questions asked. If moral people want a government of statesmen instead of a government of political parasites, a radical change must be made to America's political system.

12

Our Money or the Government's Money?

Principle Number 9: *Government has no legitimate role to play in selecting or manipulating society's money.*

God commands His people not to steal because it is immoral for one person to deprive another person of the fruits of his labor. The question then arises, "If it is wrong for one person to steal from another person, is it permissible for government to steal from individuals?" In modern society, government uses its monopoly on society's money, its "legal" ability to print unsound money that causes inflation, to steal wealth from the productive elements of society. Is this morally acceptable? Is government exempt from God's law?

Money and Freedom

Money plays an important role in any society, but its role is indispensable in a free society. This is because the free market would not operate efficiently without a reliable medium of exchange known as money. For example, without money a dairy farmer who wanted a pair of shoes would have to find a cobbler who wanted several gallons of milk—this system of barter or direct exchange is dependent on what economists call the coincidence of need. What is just as important, the dairy farmer would have no way to save his excess milk supply while he waited to find a cobbler needing milk. Money changes this situation and allows the farmer to exchange his excess milk for money in the market place and then at a later time trade the medium of exchange with a cobbler who always needs this special commodity called money. This type of exchange is referred to as indirect exchange. Money in the free market allows people to exchange their surplus output for something that every other person wants, and it also allows people to store the value of their surplus for use at a later time. This in turn allows for the accumulation of private property—capital accumulation—which enriches the free individual specifically, and society in general.

From this illustration it can be seen that in a free society all productive people are capitalists regardless of how they freely choose to earn their living. The laborer and the investment banker both accumulate private property through their own initiative. But in order for the laborer or investment banker to gain personal wealth, society's money must be "sound" money—money that does not lose its value over time.

Where Does Money Come From?

Ask most people where money comes from, and the typical response will be, "Money comes from the government." Not only is this answer wrong, but it is a wrong concept of money that is fraught with tremendous danger to individual freedom! Money arose in the free markets of antiquity as a means to facilitate exchange. In a time long forgotten and in different places at different times, free individuals found it difficult to obtain in direct exchange (barter) what they wanted. They knew intuitively that their chance of obtaining what they wanted via exchange with others would be greatly increased if they had a commodity that everyone wanted. If they exchanged their surplus for that particular commodity, they could then exchange that particular commodity, now referred to as money, with another person and thereby indirectly facilitate the exchange for the commodity that they wanted in the first place. One of the twentieth century's greatest economists and advocate of individual liberty noted that it is not reasonable to assign the development of money to government.

> ...it is difficult to conceive why one should, in dealing with the origin of indirect exchange, resort in addition to authoritarian decree or an explicit compact between citizens. A man who finds it hard to obtain in direct barter what he wants to acquire renders better his chances to acquire what he is asking for in later acts of exchange by the procurement of a more marketable good. Under these circumstances there was no need of government interference...[1]

1. Ludwig von Mises, *Human Action: A Treatise on Economics* (1949, Auburn, AL: Ludwig von Mises Institute, 1998), p. 403.

That "more marketable good" or particular commodity has been different things at different times in differing cultures. In Colonial America tobacco was occasionally used. Because tobacco was too bulky to carry around, people would store the tobacco in a warehouse and be given a receipt for the stored commodity by the warehouse owner. This receipt would then be exchanged in the market place, serving the role of "paper" money. The paper receipt in and of itself held no intrinsic value above the value of a small piece of paper, but its marketable value was in the fact that it could be exchanged for a specific amount of a known commodity. In the antebellum South cotton receipts issued by privately owned warehouses were used in similar manner. Notice that "money" under these circumstances was not the receipt but the commodity represented by the receipt. Note also that government did not issue the paper receipts—it was all a function of the free market.

Over time individuals in the free market decided that bulky and perishable commodities such as tobacco and cotton are not the best commodities to use as a medium of indirect exchange. Eventually all trading civilizations based their money on gold or silver. Gold is especially useful because it is relatively light and has high value per unit of weight. It is durable, divisible, and desirable. It is also of universal value—an ounce of gold mined in one part of the world is equal to an ounce of gold mined in another part of the world.

Sound money is based on a commonly accepted commodity. Coins are valued due to the intrinsic value of the metal making up the coin. Paper money is valued because it can be exchanged for a commodity that has intrinsic value—usually gold or silver. Under a system of sound money there is no inflation—defined as a decrease in the purchasing power of money—and there are no cycles of economic booms and busts—an overheated economy followed by recession or depression afflicting the entire nation. It should be obvious that Americans do not have a sound monetary system. The reason is simple. It is not our money; it is the government's money, money that has no intrinsic value for the forgotten man. While government money has no intrinsic value for the forgotten man, it has tremendous value (utility) for the ruling elite who control government.

What Government Did to Our Money

How did government gain control—monopolize—society's money? The answer to this question is explained by answering another question: Why do all governments seek to monopolize society's money?[2] It should be clear by now that all governments are composed, not of angels, but of fallen men who by their nature tend to feel more keenly things that affect them personally than those things that affect others. Therefore men tend to act selfishly to benefit themselves and those close to them even though it may harm others. Because government has the mystique of being legitimate, selfish men can use the "legitimate" power of government to compel those outside of the ruling elite to submit to actions that if committed outside of the cloak of government would be considered a crime. For example, if someone hacked into your bank account and stole 10 percent of the value of your account, it would be a crime. But government via inflation does this to your money every day, but it is accepted as though loss of private purchasing power was a normal part of economic life. You will never hear politicians taking the blame for the loss borne by the forgotten man, but you will often hear politicians blaming "market failures" for such losses. It is the old scheme of a robber crying "stop thief," and then escaping in the ensuing chaos.

The ruling elite of any government is a parasitic organism. The ruling elite gains its substance not from productive endeavors but by extorting a portion of the private property of productive members of society. In contemporary America it is done democratically, with the presumed consent of the governed, while such extortions are shielded with the cloak of governmental legitimacy. Kings of old learned that if subjects were taxed too heavily, these otherwise docile subjects might rise up in revolt. There is nothing worst for a king than to look out his castle window and see massive numbers of serfs with pitchforks and torches surrounding the castle seeking revenge for years of oppressive taxation.

To avoid tax revolts, kings seized control of their kingdom's money by requiring everyone to use only money bearing the king's seal. The king then would require everyone to exchange

---

2. For more information regarding sound money and the negative impact of government fiat money, see, James Ronald Kennedy, *Reclaiming Liberty* (Gretna, LA: Pelican Publishing Company, 2005), pp. 126-45.

their free-market gold coins for gold coins issued by the king's mint. The king's mint could then melt the free-market coins and dilute the gold, for example, with 10 percent of base metal.[3] By the magic of dilution the king increased his treasury by the value of 10 percent; and it was all done without the serfs having to bear the weight of additional taxes. While this works out to the benefit of the king, the forgotten man (represented by the poor serfs in our example), as always when it comes to government actions, eventually bears the costs. It does not take long for people to learn that the coins they now hold contain 10 percent less gold, and therefore the purchasing power of their money is 10 percent less than it was before the king seized their free-market money. The forgotten man must now engage in commerce with money that has decreased in value. The forgotten man is being systematically robbed by government of the purchasing power of his money. Because it is "his" government doing the robbing, he is powerless to prevent it. The king has substituted inflation for taxation. The king could not do this if he had allowed the free market to continue determining the nature of money and its relative value to other commodities. The king must monopolize society's money in order to rob his subjects—government money is established not to aid commerce or to benefit the people engaged in commerce, but to allow government to extort via inflation the forgotten man's private property.

Government soon learned that collecting and melting coins, while effective, is labor intensive and costly. There is also a physical limit on how much government can dilute a gold coin with base metal before the serfs pick up the pitchforks and torches and surround the castle. The advent of paper money provided government with a new and much more effective way to gain resources via inflation. Originally, in the free market, paper money was in fact nothing more than warehouse receipts for a given commodity that the holder (bearer) could redeem for the

3. The Bible warns against evil kings (governments) that try to trick their people by diluting the silver with "dross" or impurities that add bulk but not value to the kingdom's coins. (See Isaiah 1:21-23.)

face value at any time simply by presenting the receipt (money) to the warehouse that issued the receipt. By monopolizing society's money, government became the only "legal" source for paper money. Then when government wanted more "money" to fund government projects, all it needed to do was to turn on the printing press and create "money" out of thin air!

Money with nothing to back it except the dictate of government is known as fiat money. Again, just like melting gold coins and diluting the pure gold with base metal, money created out of thin air worked well for those who had first use of the fiat money—the ruling elite. But as the new money worked its way through the economy people learned that its relative value was less than the money that was in use prior to the dumping of new money into the economy by government—government money's purchasing power had decreased.

When fiat money's purchasing power decreases, people notice it because the price they pay for items they purchase increases for no apparent reason. In the free market, price for a given item will increase when demand for it increases before producers have an opportunity to increase the supply of the item, or if there is an increase in the quality of the item that allows producers to demand a higher price. Such increase in price is not inflation, and it is usually temporary. The natural tendency of the free market is for prices to decrease. Remember how much a microwave oven cost when they first came out? Compare that to what one costs today![4] Price has gone down, and quality has gone up! This is the free market in action.

Politicians attempt to hide the cost of government-induced inflation by blaming "market failures," or the "greed of evil capitalists," or "price gouging" by unscrupulous business people. Remember inflation is not increasing price—increasing price is the symptom of inflation, not the cause. Inflation is a decrease in the purchasing power of government-monopolized money—this

---

4. The comparison is made difficult because it is necessary to take into account the effect of years of inflation by using what economists call constant dollars—expressing yesterday's price in today's money, considering the loss of purchasing power from then to now.

gives a whole new perspective to the term "monopoly money."

Sound Money and Private Property

When individuals are free to voluntarily engage in exchange, the result is a net increase in social well-being and social wealth. Money was originally established by the free market to facilitate voluntary exchange between individuals. Voluntary exchange between individuals in the free market always produces winners on both sides of the exchange (or else the exchange would not occur). Government's interference in the free market always creates winners and losers. When government is involved, the winners will always be politicians and those closely associated with politicians—a parasitic group referred to as the ruling elite. The losers will be the productive people, the numerical minority, who have no connections to government—referred to as the forgotten man. The purpose of sound money is to facilitate voluntary exchange. This stands in sharp contrast to the purpose of fiat money, which is to facilitate the extraction of wealth from the productive element of society and to redistribute it to the parasitic elements of society.

Americans will never be free until "we the people" control, through the free market, our money. Thomas Jefferson warned that commercial and especially banking interests who sought to use the Federal government to stimulate economic development were actually working to foist upon America

> ...a single and splendid government of an aristocracy, founded on banking institutions, and moneyed incorporations under the guise and cloak of their favored branches of manufactures, commerce and navigation, riding and ruling over the plundered ploughman and beggared yeomanry.[5]

Karl Marx writing in the 1840s urged his socialist followers to work for "a centralization of credit in the hands of the state, by means of a national bank with state capital and an exclusive monopoly..."[6]

---

5. Thomas Jefferson, as cited in, James R. Kennedy and Walter D. Kennedy, *Was Jefferson Davis Right?* (Gretna, LA: Pelican Publishing Company, 1998), p. 219.
6. Karl Marx, as cited in *The Free Market*, Vol. 27, No. 1, January 2009, p. 4.

Freedom cannot endure when society's money is controlled by the ruling elite. Failure to understand the logic behind the principle that government has no legitimate role to play in selecting or manipulating society's money grants the ruling elite the presumed right to deprive free individuals of their private property—limited only to the degree of greed in government.

May God help us!

13

Legitimate Government

Principle Number 10: *The only legitimate role for the Federal government is to protect private property, facilitate free trade between the sovereign states, and protect national borders.*

Minimal Government Means Minimal Opportunity for Oppression

Christians understand that worship is the most important thing we do. But even men who profess to be "free" of religious dogma will create something to worship, even if it is god-government. God created man, giving him a desire to worship. God-fearing men worship God, whereas pagan men create false gods to adore, honor, and pay homage to—and one of the greatest of these false gods is government. Those who are enamored with god-government can dream up an unlimited number of reasons to use government to extort OPM and then spend it on their favored government projects or programs. For those who worship at the altar of god-government, resistance to the expansion of government is tantamount to heresy. The politically correct media will brand those who oppose expansion of government programs as greedy, selfish, or uncaring rich business people. Nominal socialists[1] view the world as being composed of the "haves" and the "have-nots." The "haves" are those who allegedly obtained their wealth by a system of capitalist oppression of the poor, and the "have-nots"

---

1. The term "nominal socialists" is used to describe those individuals who want to use the power of government to redistribute wealth from the "rich" in society and give it via government programs and projects to the "poor." Nominal socialists never provide a definition of "rich" or "poor." Generally the rich means anyone that government can tax to gain OPM, and the poor means those who provide votes for nominal socialist candidates. Nominal socialists include Fabian socialists, liberals, and conservatives who willingly use government programs in an attempt to outbid liberals for the votes of those who receive government benefits.

are those who were, allegedly, made poor or kept poor due to the unfair and cruel capitalist system. Nominal socialists have a utopian view of society and are determined to redeem man by correcting flaws in society via government interventions, programs, and laws enforced by the police power of government. When pressed to explain their view of man—which seldom happens in the current politically correct environment—nominal socialists proclaim that man is not inherently evil and that any evil he may commit is due to social conditions (environmental factors) beyond his control. Therefore it is the duty of society, those who are not so unfortunate, to surrender to government a portion of their wealth to be used by government to perfect the unfortunate. Perfection is politically defined, and therefore is not based on any absolute moral values. Poverty is likewise politically defined, and therefore its parameters are always changing to the effect that poverty is never resolved. When a government is based on a political ideology embraced by nominal socialists, that government will continually increase its oppressive tendency. Each year it will seize more and more OPM via taxes and inflation while oppressing the liberty of its subjects with burdensome rules, regulations, laws, and court orders.

Why Men Need Government

As was discussed in chapter 3, in the beginning God created a perfect man and placed him in a perfect environment. Sin entered into the world and man fell from his original state of perfection. This fallen nature evidences itself in man's tendency[2] to do evil; to feel more keenly that which affects him than that which affects others; and to be selfish in his dealing with others; all of which results in man's tendency to be in conflict with his fellows. Man established

---

2. By acknowledging man's tendency to do evil, such as commit criminal acts, we do not mean to imply that fallen man cannot control this tendency. The fact is that while all men have the tendency to do evil, most are moral and with God's help are able to resist the tendency. A few do not wish to follow the example set by the moral element in society, and when they yield to the tendency to do evil and commit crime, government has the duty to step in and punish them. Punishment, because it is deserved, may deter further acts by those individuals, and it will serve to warn others and therefore re-enforce their desire to discipline themselves by resisting the temptation to do evil and thereby avoid the punishment imposed by society.

government out of necessity to have an independent referee to control and punish those who could not or would not control and discipline themselves. Because man is imperfect his creations will be stained with imperfection. And so it is with government— even the best intentions of man to create a fair and just system of government will eventually be defeated due to man's sinful nature. Selfish men will seize government and use its powers for personal aggrandizement. The founding fathers of this country knew this fact and sought to limit this danger by establishing a republic of republics with a written constitution that specifically limited the role of the national[3] (federal) government. The founding fathers knew that the smaller the government the less the likelihood it would become oppressive and the greater the probability that "we the people" will be able to maintain individual liberty and freedom.

The Role of Government

Two of the many passions afflicting humanity are envy and covetousness. Man has a tendency to want things that do not belong to him. Government can do nothing to remove the sinful nature in man—failure of nominal socialists to understand this fact is the root of much of their misguided (perhaps even well-intended) government programs. Government does have a legitimate role to play in preventing those men who cannot or will not discipline themselves from stealing private property. The protection of private property is an incontestable role for government in a free society. Most of the protection will be provided at the local and state level. The national (federal) government has a very limited role to play, usually based on conflicts between citizens of two different sovereign states—referred to in constitutional dicta as diversity of citizenship—or when a criminal act occurs on federal property.

3. We use the term "national" for convenience of the reader. Actually the original constitution did not create a "nation" in the sense of a supreme nation-state as known in Europe. The founding fathers created a republic of republics in which "we the people" at the local level made the vast majority of decisions regarding our governance while reserving the right, via our sovereign state, to cancel any Federal act that "we the people" of the sovereign state felt violated those constitutional rights plainly and specifically reserved to the sovereign state and the people thereof.

In addition to protecting private property from criminal acts, government provides a means to adjudicate civil conflicts such as the enforcement of contracts. Because this role has been well established since the inception of the United States, and even earlier during the colonial era, most people take it for granted. But not every country is so lucky (blessed), and as a result the people of those countries suffer great poverty. Their poverty is due to the failure of their government to adequately perform its most basic role. Politically correct nominal socialists routinely ignore this fundamental cause of poverty. One authority noted the fact that lack of adequate protection for private property in Latin America is a major cause of the systemic poverty suffered by the masses living there. Note that poverty is a result of the failure of government to fulfill its primary role. Poverty is not the result of the exploitations of greedy capitalists. Empirical evidence was noted to prove the point.

> Recent studies have concluded that GDP [Gross Domestic Product] per capita is twice as high in nations with the strongest protections of property ($23,796) as in those providing only a moderate amount of protection ($13,027). By the same token, in those countries where there is little protection, GDP per capita drops considerably ($4,963).[4]

It should be obvious that even in primitive society man needs to accumulate private property to help him acquire those things necessary for his survival. As individuals accumulate more private property, social wealth increases, which raises the standard of living of everyone in that society. If private property is not protected, men will not be able to increase their productive output, and society will stagnate and die. Failure to protect private property serves as a disincentive to productive activity. A rational man will see no reason to exert himself to develop new tools or produce more goods if he knows that there is a high probability that the fruits of his labors will be taken away from him. Security of private property is absolutely essential for man's survival and improvement. Government's role is

---

4. Alvaro Vargas Llosa, "The Case of Latin America," *Making Poor Nations Rich*, Benjamin Powell, ed. (Stanford, CA: Stanford University Press, 2008), pp. 193-94.

to protect private property from those who would live parasitically by stealing from productive people. Pointing out the natural tendency to societal improvement by protecting private property demonstrates why even non-Bible believing people should respect the Ten Commandments.

Unfortunately, parasitic individuals are clever enough to realize that stealing outside the law is far more dangerous than seizing control of government and using its "legitimacy" to follow a parasitic lifestyle by "legally" stealing from the productive members of society. The disincentive to be productive occurs regardless of whether the one removing private property is a criminal or a government tax collector. It is a very common practice of American taxpayers to lament, "Why should I work more? Most of my extra earnings go to pay income taxes." Big government via taxes, inflation, and burdensome rules and regulations reduces American productivity and entrepreneurial activities and gradually almost imperceptibly reduces free and self-sufficient individuals to government dependents.

An important role for the Federal government in our original republic of republics was to encourage voluntary exchange between citizens of the various states. The main deficiency of the government under the Articles of Confederation, ratified by the individual states by 1781, which preceded the government created by the U.S. Constitution, was that the Articles of Confederation did not allow for a free trade zone between the states of the confederation. This discouraged commerce, which in turn decreased the opportunity for citizens to increase their personal wealth. As a result, social wealth did not increase as much as it could have if free exchange among citizens of various states had been allowed. Such problems gave rise to the Annapolis Convention (1786), which set in motion the activities that resulted in the Constitutional Convention (1787), which gave birth to the new constitution that was submitted to the states that year. Most of the delegates who attended these meetings would have been satisfied with merely amending the Articles of Confederation to allow for free trade among the states. Other elements intervened, especially those who followed the monarchist theory of government advocated by Alexander Hamilton, and an initial push for a centralized, supreme national government proceeded. Fortunately, the advocates for a supreme federal government were initially defeated as a result of the alarm raised by the anti-federalists such as Patrick Henry of Virginia.[5] Unfortunately those who wanted a big and powerful government never ceased their efforts to enlarge the powers of the Federal government and eventually were completely successful.

The most obvious reason for the existence of the Federal government is to provide protection from foreign enemies. The world is ruled by governments that for the most part are aggressive abroad and despotic at home. Even "democratic" governments can engage in imperialistic wars of aggression. The phrase "aggressive abroad and despotic at home" was used by General Robert E. Lee after the South's failure in the War for Southern Independence to describe the ultimate perversion of the American system if the Federal government was allowed to maintain its supremacy over the sovereign states.[6] The founding fathers knew that a single state standing alone would present a very tempting target for an aggressive foreign power. Therefore the states leagued together for the purpose of mutual protection. Unfortunately, under the current political system the Federal government refuses to perform its constitutional duty of defending the borders. Failure to prevent illegal immigration across the border between Mexico and the United States has resulted in a tremendous loss to American citizens as a result of crime committed by illegal aliens and the large cost imposed on local social services as a result of the Federal government's mandate that said services must be freely provided to illegal aliens. The current political system in America has been perverted into a government that will not do the things it is legitimately empowered to do while it brutally infringes on the reserved rights of the sovereign states and the people thereof by doing things it has no constitutional authority to do.

5. See James Ronald Kennedy and Walter Donald Kennedy, *Why Not Freedom!* (Gretna, LA: Pelican Publishing Company, 1995), pp. 28, 31, 82, 188, 206, 294.

6. Robert E. Lee, as cited in, James Ronald Kennedy and Walter Donald Kennedy, *The South Was Right!* (Gretna, LA: Pelican Publishing Company, 1994), p. 41.

Section III

Godly Republic Lost—
Godly Republic Regained

14

Politicians—America's Greatest Threat to Individual Liberty

Politicians will always find socially appealing reasons for spending other people's money, and said spending will always benefit politicians and those closely associated with them.

The Kennedy Twins' Law of Taxation

It is very seldom that a free people lose their liberty to foreign invaders. Although it is very dramatic when it occurs, in actuality it happens relatively few times in human history. In most cases when a free people lose their liberty, it is not lost to a foreign tyrant but to a domestic tyrant! In too many cases the people sit idly by and with astounding apathy watch as an Adolf Hitler or a Vladimir Lenin destroys their liberty. Christians should know that evil never approaches with an ugly face; it is always beautiful and seductive, offering something that man innately desires—peace, security, or free health care. As it has often been said, "All that is necessary for evil to triumph is for good people to do nothing."

Taxes, Politicians, and "We the People"
The law of taxation seems to question the character of democratically elected public officials—indeed upon further reflection it appears to question whether citizens should trust any government, even democratically elected government. The law of taxation does not question the character of politicians; it merely acknowledges the flawed nature of humanity—a flaw that has existed since the fall of man in the Garden of Eden. The impersonal exercise of governmental power magnifies the human tendency for evil. Thus we see the twentieth century not as a time of universal enlightenment, peace, and human understanding, but as a century of blood, rivers of blood all filled by the impersonal workings of governments directed by men such as Stalin, Lenin, Hitler, Mussolini, Mao, and Pol Pot. Even the popular American

god "democracy" does not and cannot change the nature of man and the subsequent drive of those who control government to abuse their powers to the detriment of "we the people."

Threats to Individual Liberty

A healthy respect for the inherent dangers to liberty and property posed by government was the key ingredient in the establishment of the original American Republic. Thomas Jefferson (circa 1787) warned: "In every government on earth is some trace of human weakness, some germ of corruption and degeneracy, which cunning will discover, and weakness insensibly open, cultivate, and improve. Every government degenerates when trusted to the rulers of the people alone."[1] Jefferson understood that government would "insensibly" (without people noticing or understanding) expand its power to encroach upon the liberty and property of its unfortunate subjects; slowly "at first while the spirit of the people is up, but in practice but as fast" when the people "relax" their guard. Nor did Jefferson think, as too many contemporary Americans think, that there are especially trustworthy people (politicians) who can be found through the process of democratic elections. Contemporary Americans act as though these democratically identified special people will magically put aside their sinful nature and self-interest, thus becoming naturally good leaders and rulers. Even Jefferson acknowledged that he was subject to this great fatal flaw of democratically elected government: "If once they [the people] become inattentive to the public affairs, you and I, and Congress, and Assemblies, judges, and governors shall become as wolves."[2] Americans today would do well to heed Jefferson's warning about the sheer folly of expecting that "we the people" will be able to protect our property and liberty from the encroachments of government simply by electing "good" people to public office. It is as unnatural for politicians to limit their power as it is unnatural for a rattlesnake to refrain from striking its prey.

---

1. Thomas Jefferson, as cited in, James R. Kennedy and Walter D. Kennedy, *Was Jefferson Davis Right?* (Gretna, LA: Pelican Publishing Company, 1998), p. 223.
    2. Ibid.

James Madison (circa 1787), who is often referred to as the Father of the Constitution, noted the risk to liberty that naturally arises when men establish governments. He warned that government created by men must be controlled. "If angels were to govern men, neither external nor internal controls on government would be necessary."[3] Because men are not angels, the human motivation to promote self-interest is greater than the motive to do public good. Politicians (even democratically elected politicians) will always seek their own interest first, but they will do so behind a smoke screen of "public good," "socially necessary services," "general welfare," or some other actual or supposed "moral imperative."

Former U.S. vice president and U.S. senator John C. Calhoun (circa 1840) described the tendency of social man to be more concerned about his personal improvement than the good of those who elected him; "… he is so constituted, that his direct or individual affections are stronger than his sympathetic or social feelings…But that constitution of our nature which makes us feel more intensely what affects us directly than what affects us indirectly through others, necessarily leads to conflict between individuals."[4]

Our founding fathers and leading American statesmen acknowledged the tendency in man, when invested with the administration of the impersonal power of government, to abuse those powers for his benefit and the benefit of those closely connected to him. But the aggrandizement of the politician's power, prestige, and perks of power all come at the expense and detriment of the liberty and property of "we the people." What is it about our current political system that makes it so likely to be abused to the detriment of "we the people?"

Productive Social Activities

There once was a time when rugged individualism, personal accountability, and individual self-reliance were terms commonly used to describe freedom-loving Americans. That was a time

---

3. Ibid.

4. John C. Calhoun, "A Disquisition on Government," *The Works of John C. Calhoun, Vol. I* (New York: D. Appleton and Company, MDCCLIV), pp. 3, 4.

before all manner of "good" government safety nets were enacted and funded with tax monies collected by local, state, and federal governments. There was a time when Americans did not demand that government provide "us" with economic bailouts, social safety nets, armies of social workers and bureaucrats to manage government programs, innumerable and incomprehensible rules, regulations, and court edicts. There was a time when people proudly possessed the pioneer spirit that built the freest and most prosperous nation on earth. It was *not* a time of wealth and public services trickling down to impoverished, beleaguered serfs and peasants. It was a time of wealth expanding across the population. Yes, the wealth expanded across the population in unequal proportions according to individual merit and ability and occasionally a mixture of plain luck. It was a time when productive entrepreneurs created wealth in the finest free-market tradition. They created this wealth by offering consumers goods and services with increasing quality and decreasing price. It was a time when productive people engaged in voluntary exchange in the free market, and this exchange benefited *both* parties. It was a time when families, extended families, and local communities supported and encouraged productive self-reliance. The enormous growth and resultant forced intrusion of government into previously private human social activities has all but destroyed this pioneer spirit—the spirit of productive entrepreneurs—and injected the pernicious pathology of parasitic political entrepreneurialism into American society.

Parasitic Political Activity

Politicians cannot survive in the free market. Their natural aversion to the rigors of competition, the necessity to constantly lower price while improving quality, and the requirement that all activities be voluntary and mutually beneficial—all such free-market strictures are beyond the capabilities of the political system and run counter to the natural tendency of those holding political power. The very essence and the driving force of today's politics is the ultimate reliance on force to compel private citizens to "stand and deliver" their property via taxation, regulations, and other government edicts. Politicians do not produce, they destroy! Politicians seize and redistribute wealth, and if allowed to grow unchecked they eventually destroy the very free-market system that productive people use to create wealth. Politicians are parasitic entrepreneurs. They are very skilled and crafty at what they do. They are highly driven, motivated, and crafty people who use the compulsive power of government to benefit themselves and those close to or associated with government. But be assured that in a democracy all such political activity will be skillfully draped and hidden in socially necessary reasons for extorting wealth from the productive public—after all, they will assure us, politicians are merely elected public servants. They claim they are only doing what we told them to do via the last democratically conducted election—it is not their fault, they are quick to tell citizens, that it costs so much to provide services *"demanded by the voters."* In other words it is the fault of "we the people" that politicians are compelled to take so much of our wealth for "public" services. To be honest, there is a grain of truth to this trite political excuse. In our current political system "we the people" have very little control once the election is over—the elected tell the public what the people need, how much, what quality, and at what price. Such a system provides a very convenient and effective smoke screen behind which unimaginable, self-interest promoting political deals may be quietly brokered out of sight of John and Jane Q. Public.

In a democracy such as we have today, society is divided into productive and parasitic people. Productive people are those who take care of themselves, their immediate and extended families, and the local community that nurtures and protects their liberty, property, and cultural and moral values. The unorganized mass of productive people make up the majority of citizens who during a disaster or economic downturn take care of themselves without first looking to government. Productive people are possessed with the pioneer spirit that encourages them to forgo immediate gratification and save for future uncertainties or personal dreams and hopes of the future. Their savings, which represent their conscious efforts to sacrifice today in order to plan for the future, allows them to accumulate the skills, habits, and resources to actualize their dreams for a better future or see them through unexpected disasters or economic hard times. By saving or investing (which is a form of saving) a portion of their earned income (as opposed to spending to achieve temporary instant gratification), productive people contribute to the creation of a pool of capital that is then made available to other productive entrepreneurs (business people, capitalists) who use this capital to create more, better, and less expensive goods and services—not to mention creating numerous new jobs in the process. Productive people create wealth—unfortunately, some see this wealth not as a blessing to society but as an opportunity to enrich themselves.

Political Monopolies and Special Interests

Parasitic people are also entrepreneurs, but not wealth-creating entrepreneurs. Parasitic entrepreneurs consume, distort, and destroy wealth. When productive people engage in voluntary exchange in the free market, *both* parties to the exchange gain. By injecting parasitic entrepreneurs into the social equation, government creates a situation in which one party, the parasite, gains, and the other party, productive people, lose. This situation is established in a democracy because politicians who control government, and those closely associated with the ruling elite, are highly organized around the principle of mutual self-interest, while "we the people" are unorganized and less powerful even though, at times, we may even represent the majority. Political parasites are able to use the impersonal power of government to compel productive people via force or threats of force to surrender portions of their wealth—all done of course very democratically and for the public good—the political ruling elite, after all, claim to know better than "we the people" what is really good for us.

Monopoly is an example of government-sponsored parasitic activity. Monopolies cannot exist without the aid of government. In exchange for undisclosed favors, politicians grant parasitic entrepreneurs protection from competition by granting exclusive licenses and passing laws and regulations that prevent or inhibit competitors from entering the monopolists' exclusive market. "We the people" as consumers are forced to pay higher prices and accept lower quality for goods and services by this political action. Consumers have no recourse when dealing with monopolies—after all, the forgotten man has learned through bitter experience, "You can't fight city hall."

The events surrounding 9-11 and Katrina are examples of how parasitic government can use its failure to justify more taxation to correct catastrophic government failures. In the free market of productive entrepreneurs, if an enterprise fails it is punished by economic loss and even bankruptcy. But in the parasitic world of government, if an enterprise fails—as government did in both of these cases—it is rewarded with larger shares of other people's money (OPM) forcefully extorted from "we the people" via taxation and the promise that "we will do better next time." The 2008 economic meltdown is another example of how the parasitic government that caused the distortion in the market that produced the economic meltdown was given more than $800,000,000,000 to fix a problem that it originally created! Parasites do not fix problems—political parasites use OPM to create problems and then demand even more OPM to fix the problem they created. A free society cannot long endure under such circumstances.

Americans will never reclaim their liberty and establish a moral community as long as they look to politicians for the redemption of moral society. In chapters 15 through 19 we will discuss the founding fathers' original intentions to establish a limited form of government that would support Christian moral values. In chapter 20 we provide an outline of how "we the people" can establish a legitimate, minimal government that will allow for the development and security of moral communities in those states that desire to separate themselves from the unholy things of the world.

15

Freedom—America's
Founding Fathers' Legacy

"The first thing I have at heart is American liberty, the second thing is American Union."

Patrick Henry

America's founding fathers were dedicated to the idea that men were granted inalienable rights, not from governments or kings, but from God. Because freedom is a gift from God, it cannot be encumbered by government without the consent of those who freely choose to live under that government. The right of man to *consent* to the form of government he lives under was not a commonly held idea in 1776. It is an idea that remains true today even though many who dominate or have close ties with those who control America's government no longer subscribe to the tenets of freedom as a God-given right. Today's politically correct crowd believes in a society in which government can use force to redeem man by remaking his social, cultural, and economic environment. Today's ruling elite are a stark contrast to America's moral founding fathers who knew that first and foremost man needed spiritual redemption. The founding fathers knew that liberty could not long exist outside of a moral community.

America's Christian Heritage

The first successful English settlers in America, at Jamestown, Virginia (1607), came in search of an opportunity to develop personal wealth that was denied to them in pre-industrial revolution England.[1] They brought with them a long and firm tradition of

---

1. Most Americans incorrectly think of the Pilgrims who landed at Plymouth Rock in Massachusetts as being the "first" English settlers. The Pilgrims actually landed in 1620, thirteen years after the establishment of Jamestown, Virginia. Interestingly the rivalry and radically differing view of society between the "descendants" of the Pilgrims in New England and the "descendants" of the Virginians (Southerners and inhabitants of the non-Southern "Bible Belt" states) would continue even to this day—as explained in chapter 18, "Red States Versus Blue States."

government and religious faith. The "Rights of Englishmen," such as the prohibition of taxation without representation, would eventually become a rallying cry for American independence. The Christian faith of the first settlers would give them the personal assurance of the protection of Divine Providence as they sought to establish civilization in a strange and dangerous land. In many respects this would be the first time in history, other than the time Joshua led the Israelites into the Promised Land, when a people would establish a new nation based on ideas of limited government, protection of private property rights, and firm religious faith.

Secular humanists have attacked the notion that America was established by people with firm Christian values. They allege that America's founding fathers were a diverse group of deists and religious dissenters who wanted a "wall of separation" between religious faith and anything dealing with government—which of course means everything outside of the walls of churches. While no religious litmus test is demanded in the United States Constitution, every state constitution recognized God as central in the life of the state or colony. For example, the Charter of Rhode Island, which predates the United States Constitution by more than one hundred years, proclaims: "That they [the colonists of Rhode Island], pursuing with peace and loyal minds their sober, serious, and religious intentions, of Godly edifying themselves and one another in the holy Christian faith and worship...."[2] In the Massachusetts Declaration of Rights it is clearly stated that "It is the right, *as well as the duty*, of all men in society, publicly, and at stated seasons, to worship the Supreme Being, the Great Creator and Preserver of the universe."[3] [Emphasis added.] In the Constitution of South Carolina we read the following, "The free exercise and enjoyment of religious profession and worship without discrimination or preference, shall for ever hereafter, be allowed within this state to all mankind."[4] These are just a few examples that could be taken from any of the Original Thirteen Colonies or states. It

---

2. See the chapter on Rhode Island in Moore and Lake, *The American's Guide to the Constitution of the United States of America* (Trenton, NJ:1813), p. 101.

3. The Constitution of Massachusetts, as cited in, ibid., p. 69.

4. The Constitution of South Carolina, as cited in, ibid., p. 242.

should be noted that these statements were made before the United States Constitution was written. The very delegates who wrote and ratified the U.S. Constitution understood that this language was in the constitutions of their states. Even after the adoption of the U.S. Constitution, God was recognized in the constitutions of new states as they were admitted to the Union. In 1796 Tennessee was added to the Union. Tennessee demanded that anyone holding office in Tennessee must have faith in God: "No person who denies the being of God or a future state of rewards and punishment shall hold office in the civil department of this state."[5] Most new states added to the Union had similar requirements in their constitutions, and these constitutions had to be approved by the delegates of the other states in Congress. In the early days of America, and even down to the last few decades in contemporary America, religious faith based on biblical principles was a given—atheists, agnostics, universalists, and non-God fearers as social leaders were virtually unknown. Yet, modern Americans have been 'brainwashed" by secular humanists and their allies in government, universities, and the liberal media into believing that a few references to deist thought by less than 5 percent of America's founding fathers is the total picture of America's religious heritage! Dr. M. E. Bradford noted this fallacy:

> As I have come to know through my own work, the concept of the Framers as ordinary Christians, as members in good standing of the various Christian communions found in early America, is supported by the recorded patterns of their lives...The assumption that this majority was likely to agree to totally secular institutional arrangements in the very structure of American politics contradicts almost everything we know about human nature, as well as the most self-evident components of Christian teaching concerning the relation of the magistrate to the ultimate source of his authority in God.[6]

Dr. Bradford then provided evidence of the Christian faith of well-known leaders of the American Revolution to support the

---

5. The Constitution of Tennessee, as cited in, ibid., p. 342.

6. M. E. Bradford, *Original Intentions: On the Making and Ratification of the United States Constitution* (Athens, GA: The University Press of Georgia, 1993), pp. 88-89.

once common belief in the faith of our fathers. Patrick Henry of Virginia declared in his last will and testament: "This is all the inheritance I can give to my dear family. The religion of Christ will give them one which will make them rich indeed."[7] John Jay of New York declared in his last will and testament: "Unto Him who is the author and giver of all good I render sincere and humble thanks for His merciful and unmerited blessings, and especially for our redemption and salvation by his beloved Son."[8] George Mason, of Virginia, left us this testament: "My soul I resign into the hands of my Almighty Creator…thro the merits of my blessed Savior for a remission of sins."[9] To claim, as secular humanists do, that America was not established as a Christian nation is to ignore plain facts in order to foist an immoral governmental system upon American society. There is no doubt that early American leaders did not want and fervently sought to avoid the possibility of an official national religion. But separation of the national authority (the Federal government) from, and the prevention of, the establishment of a national religion is far different from what has been foisted upon moral Americans today—the expulsion of the Christian faith and values from the "public" sphere.

America's First Experiment with Freedom

It is of vital importance for those who want to reestablish moral communities in America to first understand the origins of moral and free communities in America. The Original Thirteen American Colonies were not founded *en masse* (all together at once). Each colony had its own separate founding; its separate beginnings were not directly connected to any other colony; and most important, its internal governance was not connected to any other colony. Each American colony had slightly different motivations for its establishment, slightly different populations, slightly different forms of dominant Christian religion, and slightly different mechanisms for governing the colony. The two connecting thoughts or ideas were the idea of the "Rights of

7. Ibid.
8. Ibid., 89-90.
9. Ibid.

Englishmen" and their firm Christian faith. Each colony looked to England, with its developing heritage of individual freedom, as its source of political authority and to the Christian faith as its source of a social code of moral conduct.

When the Original Thirteen American Colonies declared their independence, they did so as individual (sovereign) states acting together to establish and successfully maintain their newly declared independence. The Declaration of Independence of July 4, 1776, was a joint act that merely codified the separate act of each colony by withdrawing its consent (seceding) from its union with Great Britain.[10] The words used in this great declaration were not chosen lightly. Notice how the declaration plainly states that "...these United Colonies" are free; note the plural. The signers of the Declaration of Independence were not announcing the founding of a single free and independent nation, but the freedom and independence of each individual colony. The declaration continues by announcing to the world that these former colonies were now "Free and independent States." Note once again the use of the plural "States."

After a long and arduous struggle by the colonists, God blessed America with victory over an empire that dominated the world of its day. The fact that a handful of insignificant colonies were able to wrest liberty from a world empire is, in and of itself, firm evidence that God had a hand in the establishment of and a purpose for this new country. Great Britain was forced to acknowledge the independence of its former American colonies by signing the Treaty of Paris in 1783. In the treaty that formally recognized American independence, Great Britain recognized not the independence of the United States, but the independence of each former colony individually by name! These former dependent colonies became free, independent, and sovereign states. From that day to this day, nowhere in any formal or informal document can it be found where these free, independent, and sovereign states renounced their freedom, independence, or sovereignty! There is no place in American history where the

10. In May of 1776 the colony of Virginia had already declared that "...the union which has hitherto subsisted between Great Britain and the American colonies is thereby totally dissolved, and that the inhabitants of *this* [emphasis added] colony are discharged from any allegiance to the crown of Great Britain."

sovereign states surrendered their inherent right to self-government or their right to protect the sovereign communities within the jurisdiction of the sovereign state from the encroachments of an aggressive and oppressive governmental force—including a Federal government ruled and controlled by secular humanists.

The fact that each colony was independent from other colonies set the stage for the eventual establishment of the original, sovereign, thirteen American states. The fact that one colony, and eventually state, might decide to require by law the attendance of church services in no way affected the rights of citizens in neighboring colonies or eventually states. Under the original American system, each independent and sovereign state was free to establish a community in accordance to the will of "we the people" within that specific state. Freedom of movement within the United States meant that if a particular state passed laws that an individual found to be oppressive, he could work to change the laws or "vote with his feet" by moving to a state whose laws were more in fitting with the individual's personal beliefs.

The government established by the Articles of Confederation (1777) made it very clear that each former colony (now state) reserved its "...sovereignty, freedom, and independence..." and all rights not "expressly delegated to the United States..." These words and the intentions of these words are repeated in the Ninth and Tenth Amendments of the U.S. Constitution that would eventually be ratified by the Original Thirteen American states. America began as a group of colonies with each colony responsible for the establishment and governance of the community within that particular colony. The history of these colonies demonstrates that the overarching desire of "we the people" within each colony was to protect their right to govern themselves in a fashion agreeable to the people within each colony. Each colony was unique with differing laws and customs, but all were united by their strong attachment to the concept of individual liberty (referred to as the "Rights of Englishmen") and their acceptance of the Christian faith as the source of morality for their communities. These principles flowed through to the establishment of the Federal government under the Original Constitution.

America's First Tax Revolt

The political concept of a tax revolt is well ingrained in the

American political tradition. It might come as a surprise that it is neither a new nor uniquely American concept. In ancient Mesopotamia around 2400 BC a man named Urukagina led a revolt against the ruling elite composed of religious and political leaders who were extracting wealth from private citizens for the benefit of the ruling elite and those with close connections to the ruling elite.[11] As we have already noted in chapter 3, God warned His people about the dangers to individual freedom and private property posed by big government. The American experience during the colonial era re-enforced this concern and made Americans during the colonial and initial postcolonial period very skeptical of government and those closely allied or connected with those in control of government.

The citizens of Virginia revolted against Great Britain when the British king's government levied a two-pence-per-pound tax on tea sold in the colony. The people in the colony of Maine rose up against the king when his government attempted to confiscate every standing white pine tree in the colony. Every American is taught about the famous Boston Tea Party, which was an American reaction to the king's (relatively slight) increase on the cost of tea sold in the Americas. The reason tax policy is so important is that, by depriving citizens of even a "small" portion of their private property, to be used by government for projects or purposes that would not be the first choice of the taxed citizens, the result is a reduction of the private citizens' liberty. The American attitude toward unreasonable taxation is summed up by Arthur Lee of Virginia in 1775 when he declared: "The right of property is the guardian of every other right, and to deprive the people of this, is in fact to deprive them of their liberty."[12] Recall in chapter 4 we noted that a people cannot be free without private property. As government hinders or confiscates private property, it decreases individual liberty and slowly (insidiously) transforms free citizens into dependent slaves.

11. Alvaro Vargas Llosa, "The Case of Latin America," *Making Poor Nations Rich*, Benjamin Powell, ed. (Stanford, CA: Stanford University Press, 2008), p. 189.

12. As cited in H. L. Mencken, *Prejudices*, 2nd Series (New York: Knopf, 1924), p. 221.

At the end of the War for American Independence, King George did not grant liberty to Americans *en masse,* nor was it granted to the United States as a national unity. Freedom was granted to each sovereign state, said state acting as the corporate representative of "we the people" within each respective sovereign community. Freedom in America arises from the people, who authorize their corporate representative, the sovereign state, to act on their behalf. The sovereign states then created their representative or agent, the Federal government, by delegating (as opposed to surrendering) a portion of their state's authority in order for their agent, the Federal government, to perform those limited and specific functions that the states acting individually could not efficiently perform. The limited nature of the Federal government was meant to reduce the likelihood of big government oppressing the rights reserved by the sovereign states and to limit its ability to extort private property from "we the people" via a harsh tax policy. At this point every Christian should reread God's warning to Israel as they demanded a king (big government) to rule over them. The very acts of tyranny that God warned Israel a king would bring upon them is analogous to the evil of big government in America today.

16

Original Intentions
for a More Perfect Union

"We the People of the United States, in Order to form a more perfect Union... "

Preamble U.S. Constitution

When the framers of the Constitution met in Philadelphia in 1787, they did not come together as utopian dreamers seeking to perfect human society. They had specific purposes, mainly surrounding the need to allow for better commerce between the sovereign states within the confederation. The framers were very skeptical about the role of government in their communities, especially the Federal government. The framers had no desire to create one massive centralized "City on the Hill" to which private citizens would be forced to pay large sums of their private earnings. Their purpose was to craft a government to which independent-minded, God-fearing Americans were likely to give their consent. The last thing to which these moral Americans were likely to give their consent was a supreme, centralized, tax-consuming, bureaucratic government similar to the one in England from which they had so recently seceded.

God's Morality Versus God-Government's Morality

The argument made throughout this book is that: (1) man is a fallen creature needing spiritual redemption in order to be acceptable to God; (2) God requires man to earn his living by productive labor[1] and to respect the property of others;[2] (3) due to man's fallen nature he needs government to protect him from his fellows, some of whom

---

1. "In the sweat of thy face shalt thou eat bread..." (Genesis 3:19); "Six days shalt thou labor..." (Exodus 20:9).
2. See the Ten Commandments prohibitions against stealing and coveting in Exodus 20:15 & 17.

would use force to deprive other men of their property or lives; and (4) God warns man about the dangers of kings (government) and encourages His people to live as free men in a moral community presided over by a small, decentralized government.

Utopian dreamers and secular humanists deny the biblical account of man as a fallen creature needing, first and foremost, spiritual redemption. They view man as being totally perfectible by human efforts. When they see a man "in the gutter" their first thought is to change that man's environment. What tool do secular humanists use for changing the environment of the "unfortunate," the "downtrodden," or those "abused by an oppressive capitalist system"? They do not use their own private wealth; nor do they rely on their favorite charity to do their "good" work. Government force is the favorite and ultimate tool they use to correct what they perceive to be the result of social "injustice." They eagerly use the political power of government backed up by the police force of government to extort private property (usually in the form of taxes) from the productive element of society. They then use other people's money (OPM) to fund government social workers/bureaucrats who are paid by the ruling elite to manage govern-ment programs that are supposed to help the "victims" of a "cruel" and "unjust" society. The fact that these government programs seldom, if ever, succeed in eliminating the perceived "social injustice" is never acknowledged or discussed. Each year the previous year's failure is rewarded by an even larger outlay of OPM. The sad fact is that instead of eliminating actual problems these programs result in an increase in social problems. But because secular humanists are not motivated by a biblical-based moral code, they have no remorse about making a bad situation worse—after all, what is important to the secular humanists is to feel good about using government to resolve the perceived underlying problem of greed inherent in the "cruel capitalist" system. The mere fact that they have made matters worse for the "victim" or that they have stolen private property from productive citizens is of no material consequence. This is the sad reality of America's current immoral government—which is not the government the founding fathers intended to leave "we the people." Whereas Christians worship a God Who is capable of correcting the faulty nature of man, secular humanists worship governmental institutions, which they faithfully believe can change man. Central to the dichotomy of views between Christians and secular humanists is the issue of which God man should depend on and worship.

Nation-State Versus Moral Communities

When the fifty-five delegates from the states came together at the Constitutional Convention in Philadelphia in 1787, they brought many varying ideas about how to "fix" the government created by the Articles of Confederation and make the United States of America a "more perfect Union." Some, like James Madison, came with the Virginia Plan that proposed a strong centralized federal government that would dominate the states and reduce them to nothing more than mere subservient political subdivisions of an all-powerful consolidated national authority. Madison's initial plan received a harsh rebuke and subsequent to the rejection of his plan Madison emerged from the convention as one of the strongest advocates of decentralized federalism, States Right's, and government controlled primarily at the level of the state and local community. Others, such as Alexander Hamilton, came to the convention seeking a strong federal executive (president) with powers almost as regal as those of a king and a federal senate appointed for life similar to the British House of Lords. Hamilton's dreams of a dominant, centralized, supreme federal government were also rejected but, unlike Madison, Hamilton never changed his dreams for an authoritarian federal government. He spent the rest of his life working to enlarge the authority and power of the Federal government, and in many ways he was very successful. Thomas Jefferson declared that Hamilton was "not only a monarchist but a monarchist bottomed on corruption."[3] The central theme, underlying motive, and overarching question in all the debates and discussions during the Constitutional Convention was whether or not the United States would have a strong, centralized, national government that would rule "we the people" in our local communities, or would the government of the United States be a decentralized federal republic composed of sovereign states?

3. Thomas Jefferson, as cited in James R. Kennedy and Walter D. Kennedy, *Was Jefferson Davis Right?* (Gretna, LA: Pelican Publishing Company, 1998), p. 217.

A reading of the debates and discussions during the Constitutional Convention and the precise language of the original document clearly demonstrates the intentions of the founding fathers. They were determined to protect rights that had been abused by the central government of Great Britain from which they had seceded in 1776 and to create a "minimal government, directly responsive at the local level to the population that it served."[4] When Madison began pushing his plan to form a strong and centralized federal government, his co-sponsor Edmund Randolph of Virginia was quick to assure delegates such as Pierce Butler and John Rutledge of South Carolina that he had no "intention to give indefinite powers to the national legislature, declaring that he was entirely opposed to such an inroad on the state jurisdictions, and that he did not think any considerations whatever could ever change his determination."[5] The initial attempt to create a strong and dominant central government by giving the federal government the right to veto state legislation almost caused the dispersal of the Constitutional Convention.

> Gouverneur Morris, [from Pennsylvania], called the power in question "terrible to the states" and predicted it might "disgust" its opponents. John Lansing of New York described it as potentially even "more injurious" than the British government's negative over the American colonial legislatures. Roger Sherman [from Connecticut], insisted that the power they were creating should be forbidden "to interfere with the government of the individual states in any matters of local police."[6]

The idea of creating a dominant, centralized, national government soon evaporated. The delegates then set about designing a limited republic of republics—a government that "we the people" within their local communities would accept. In the words of the Declaration of Independence, the framers of the Original Constitution formed a legitimate government founded on

4. M. E. Bradford, *Original Intentions: On the Making and Ratification of the United States Constitution* (Athens, GA: The University Press of Georgia, 1993), p. xvi.

5. Ibid., p. 8.

6. Ibid., p. 10.

the "consent of the governed." The manner in which that consent was obtained is irrefutable proof that the founding fathers created a limited, federal republic of republics.

Free, Independent, and Sovereign States Ratify the Constitution

When the Constitutional Convention completed its work in September of 1787, the government of the United States was still functioning under the Articles of Confederation. The Constitution proposed to establish a new, "more perfect" government, but first this proposed new government had to receive the consent of the governed. If the framers of the Constitution had intended to establish a totally new form of government—a supreme national government—to replace the decentralized model, then a national vote would have been held to ratify the new national government. If the United States was to have a new, supreme national government, then "we the people" would have held a national vote in which the new government would have been accepted or rejected. But this did not happen—no national vote was ever held! Why? Because the form of government, a decentralized federal government, did not change; its authority was merely increased, and the right of the states to set barriers to commerce between the various members of the Union was surrendered—thus establishing a free-trade zone within the United States. If "we the people" did not vote in a national election to accept the proposed Constitution, then how was the Constitution ratified?

The United States government formed under the Articles of Confederation in no less than five places declared that government to be "perpetual." Great Britain recognized the freedom, independence, and sovereignty of its former colonies in the Treaty of Paris in 1783. These United States at that time had a federal government under the Articles of Confederation and Perpetual Union. These thirteen independent and sovereign states expressly intended to retain their sovereignty. Their sovereignty was more important than the perpetuity of their union. This is made clear in Article II of the Articles of Confederation.[7] These thirteen states

---

7. "Each state retains its sovereignty, freedom, and independence, and every power, jurisdiction and right, which is not by this Confederation expressly delegated to the United States, in Congress assembled."

then had to decide whether or not they wanted to secede from their current "Perpetual Union" under the Articles of Confederation and form a "more perfect" union under the new Constitution. Because they, as sovereign states, formed the government under the Articles of Confederation, the question of whether or not to secede from that government by forming a new government under the Constitution had to be answered—not by "we the people" *en masse* as a nation, but by "we the people" through the function of the sovereign states. But each state had to act for and only for itself—that is, for the people of the sovereign community of which that state was their corporate representative. The decision of one state to accept or reject the proposed new government in no way encumbered or compelled the decision of other states.

The source of the authority of the new government to be formed under the Constitution is found in Article VII of the Constitution. It declares: "Ratification of the Conventions of nine States shall be sufficient for the Establishment of this Constitution *between the States so ratifying the Same.*" [Emphasis added.] Article VII has two very important points for those who want to establish moral communities within these United States. First, Article VII plainly establishes that the Federal government's authority is derived from the states, and as such it is not original authority but delegated authority (authority on loan from the states); and second, in accepting or rejecting the proposed Constitution the states were acting as independent and sovereign states. Even if a constitutional majority of the other states (nine) ratified the Constitution, the actions of the majority could not bind or force acceptance on the remaining four states. According to Article VII, when nine states had voted to leave the perpetual union previously formed under the Articles of Confederation and accept the new government under the Constitution, the new government would be established—but only for those states electing to leave the old government. Indeed, the fear of the proposed government being seized by malicious factions and used against the interests of the minority was so great that Rhode Island and North Carolina did not join the new Union until well over a year after ratification of the proposed Constitution by other states. The ratification, and in many cases the uneasy ratification, was done by "we the people" acting through the sovereign state.

When the proposed Constitution was submitted to the people

for their review, it was not certain whether or not it would be accepted. Initially, the people were hesitant to empower a new government more "efficient" than the one they had under the Articles of Confederation for fear that their new government would become as oppressive as the one in Great Britain from which they had seceded in 1776. The men who were opposed to the new government were known as anti-Federalists. They were lead by such notable American patriots as Patrick Henry. Many patriotic citizens were concerned about the potential for abuse inherent in the new government due to the new taxing authority that was given to the Federal government. They foresaw a day in which a majority would capture control of the Federal government and use its taxing authority to extort money from the minority for the benefit of the majority. Patrick Henry was clear when he warned Virginians:

> [I] am sure that the dangers of this system are real, when those who have no similar interests with the people of this country [Virginia] are to legislate for us—when our dearest interests are to be left in the hands of those whose advantage it will be to infringe them.[8]

Those who supported the adoption of the Constitution were known as Federalists. The Federalists sought to allay fears about the possibility of the new Federal government becoming oppressive of State's Rights. The main body of the Federalists' arguments and assurances can be found in the *Federalist Papers*.

In most of the states there was a slight majority who favored the anti-Federalists—that is, the majority were reluctant to grant more power to the Federal government. To convince enough of the anti-Federalists to vote in favor of the Constitution, the Federalists were forced to give assurances such as "[I]t may safely be received as an axiom in our political system, that the State governments will in all possible contingencies, afford complete security against invasions of the public liberty by the national authority," and again, "[W]e

---

8. Patrick Henry, as cited in, James Ronald Kennedy and Walter Donald Kennedy, *Why Not Freedom!* (Gretna, LA: Pelican Publishing Company, 1995), p. 31.

may safely rely on the disposition of the State legislatures to erect barriers against the encroachments of the national authority."[9] But even this assurance was not enough to gain ratification of the new government. Many of the anti-Federalists were willing to support ratification only if it were amended to include a "Bill of Rights."

The first ten amendments to the Constitution are what we commonly refer to as the Bill of Rights. Even a cursory reading of these amendments will demonstrate that they are a prohibition against the Federal government! The Federal government, for example, is prohibited from establishing an official religion for the United States. The state of Connecticut, on the other hand, had an official state religion until 1816, and Massachusetts had an official state religion until 1833! The Federal Bill of Rights did not negate Connecticut's or Massachusetts' right to establish a state religion! Indeed, the Federal Supreme Court acknowledged the fact that the prohibitions against the establishment of an official religion in the Bill of Rights did not apply to the states in a ruling in 1833.[10] Eventually Connecticut and Massachusetts realized, as did all other states, that mixing religion with politics was not a good idea and rescinded their laws relative to an official religion for their state.

The Ninth and Tenth Amendments were included to make sure that the rights, independence, freedom, and sovereignty then held by the sovereign states under the Articles of Confederation would be safe under the new government. The Tenth Amendment declares that the states retain all rights not specifically delegated (loaned) to the Federal government. Just to make sure there were no misunderstandings the states used the Ninth Amendment to declare that just because a right (the right of nullification for example) is not listed—"enumerated"—in the Constitution, that would not be grounds to claim that such rights do not exist! Together the Ninth and Tenth Amendments announce to the world that the sovereign state retains its complete independence to act

9. Alexander Hamilton in *The Federalist Papers, No. 28 and No. 85.* (The authors question whether Hamilton—as evidenced by his prior statements and his subsequent actions—was sincere or merely making these statements to lure anti-Federalist votes.)

10. *Barron v. Baltimore,* 7 Peters 243 (1833).

unless a specific right is: (1) delegated to the Federal government or (2) prohibited to the states by the Constitution. The protections afforded by the first ten amendments, especially the Ninth and Tenth Amendments, convinced many anti-Federalists to support ratification, and therefore the Constitution was adopted.

But for many states even these firm assurances was not enough. The states of Virginia and New York in their ratification agreements specifically reserved the right to withdraw (secede) from the United States if the powers granted to the Federal government were used to the detriment of the people of those states. Yes, the states wanted "a more perfect Union," but not if it came at the cost of American liberty! The states understood that their role was to be the ultimate defender of their citizens' liberty against the encroachments of an oppressive Federal government. As Patrick Henry noted: "The first thing I have at heart is American *liberty*, the second thing is American *Union*."

Under the original republic of republics, the sovereign community within each state could establish a system of government that supported their community. For example, if an individual lived in Connecticut and was not a member of the official state religion, he could work to change the law (which was eventually done), or he could "vote with his feet" by moving to another state that supported his moral values. But, in contemporary America, those choices no longer exist. Americans now live in an era of the supremacy of a Federal government controlled by secular humanists. When the supreme Federal government now decides to encroach on the right of the once sovereign state to, for example, determine when life begins, there is nothing the once sovereign community can do to correct a "law" of man that the moral community feels violates its moral code. Modern Americans, unlike the citizen in Connecticut of the 1800s, cannot "vote with their feet," nor do they have a chance to change the law, because the secular humanists are ruling by majority vote at the national level. The only political solution is to regain the liberty that has been stolen from "we the people" of the sovereign community or remain forever subservient to a secular humanist, supreme national government.

17

The Struggle to Prevent
Big Government (1789-1860)

"With no more than five exceptions, they [the founding fathers] were orthodox members of one of the established Christian communions. An internal transformation of American society in the direction of a secularized egalitarian state was the furthest thing from the minds of these men."

M. E. Bradford[1]

Man's history is full of examples of the extreme struggle between good and evil. American history is no different. In America it has always been a struggle between the organized few who wanted to control government and the unorganized many who only wanted government to leave them alone. The efforts of those desiring to, as they would state it, use the power of the Federal government to improve society was evident from the beginning of this nation. As is always true with fallen man, the so-called effort to improve society was just an excuse to use the taxing and regulatory powers of big government to improve their personal fortunes.

The Struggle of Good and Evil (1789)

All Christians know that the struggle between good and evil will never be over as long as this mortal world remains—or as is often said throughout the Bible Belt and Christian communities everywhere, "Until the Lord returns in great glory." The same was true regarding the struggle to maintain local self-government with maximum liberty reserved for "we the people" of the sovereign community within each state. As noted in the previous chapter, James Madison came to the Constitutional Convention with a plan

---

1. M. E. Bradford, *Founding Fathers: Brief Lives of the Framers of the United States Constitution* (Lawrence, KS: The University Press of Kansas, 1981), p. xvi.

that would have deprived the states of their sovereignty by creating a centralized, supreme federal government. After his initial plan was soundly rejected, Madison had a dramatic change in his view of the federal government. History does not tell us what caused Madison's political "Damascus Road" conversion from federal supremacist to ardent defender of State's Rights. Somehow during the early debates Madison changed his political philosophy from an advocate of—what we would today call—big government, to an advocate of limited federalism and State's Rights. Thomas Jefferson, who was serving in France during the Constitutional Convention, would later join Madison to become America's archetypical opponents of those who wanted to enlarge the powers of the federal government and thereby became America's chief defenders of State's Rights.

Alexander Hamilton also came to the Constitutional Convention with a plan to establish a regal federal government in which the federal president would appoint the governors of each state, and United States senators would serve for life! When his plan was rejected he became so irate that he stormed out of the convention and did not return until it was almost over. While Madison had a conversion from big government to limited federalism and State's Rights; Hamilton emerged from the convention a crafty and unprincipled plotter determined to do whatever it took to enlarge the role of the Federal government. The initial struggle to preserve the original intentions of the founding fathers was essentially a battle between those who followed the Hamiltonian philosophy of enlarging Federal powers by a loose construction or reading of the Constitution (Federalists) and those who followed Madison and Jefferson who believed that Federal authority was limited to the specific grants made by the states to the Federal government by the Constitution—strict construction or reading of the Constitution (Republicans).[2]

Thomas Jefferson viewed the efforts of the Federalists as an

2. Jeffersonian Republicans should not be confused with the Republican Party that emerged in the late 1850s. The Republican Party of Abraham Lincoln was in fact a follower of the Federalist Party and believed in federal supremacy and use of government to benefit industry, commerce, and manufacturing. See Walter Donald Kennedy and Al Benson, Jr., *Red Republicans and Lincoln's Marxists* (Gretna, LA: Pelican Publishing Company, 2010).

unprincipled attempt to use the force of the Federal government to enlarge their fortunes and the fortunes of those close to the Federalist ruling elite. He recognized the attempt to misuse the government created by the founding fathers for what it was—an attempt to better those holding power by creating a government they controlled that would be:

> [A] single and splendid government of an aristocracy, founded on banking institutions, and moneyed incorporations under the guise and cloak of their favored branches of manufactures, commerce and navigation, riding and ruling over the plundered ploughman and beggared yeomanry.[3]

In his speech at his first inauguration Jefferson described the Federal government in a much smaller role as a "...frugal government that does not take from the worker the bread he has earned."[4] Jefferson's view and a view that was shared by those who supported the State's Rights strict-construction interpretation of the Constitution was that the Federal government should be so small and limited that the burden borne by the average citizen would be light, so light that it would hardly be noticed. Yet, this was not the view of the Federalists who wanted to expand the role of the Federal government even though such expansion would encroach upon the rights reserved by the sovereign states and eventually add increasing burdens to be borne by the average citizen.

Hamilton's Federal Bank and Loose Construction of the Constitution (1791)

The founding fathers were well aware of the dangers posed by government money. Their experience with paper money (Continental script) issued during the Revolutionary War taught them the meaning of American soldiers' complaint of the paper money used to pay for their services—a complaint that at one time

---

3. Thomas Jefferson, as cited in, James R. Kennedy and Walter D. Kennedy, *Was Jefferson Davis Right?* (Gretna, LA: Pelican Publishing Company, 1998), p. 219.

4. Thomas Jefferson, as cited in, James Ronald Kennedy and Walter Donald Kennedy, *Why Not Freedom!* (Gretna, LA: Pelican Publishing Company, 1994), p. 34.

was well known in America. Anything that was generally useless or worthless was described as being "not worth a Continental." Jefferson knew that banking set up and funded by government always resulted in the enrichment of the few who were close to the government banking system and the impoverishment of the many who had no close relations with the ruling elite. Therefore when Hamilton purposed to President George Washington a federal banking system to encourage commercial development, Jefferson urged President Washington to resist the creation of this new Federal power. Jefferson declared that the Federal government was not authorized by the plain language of the Constitution to enter into the business of banking.

Hamilton countered Jefferson's strict-construction argument by offering for the first time the loose-construction argument. According to Hamilton, the Constitution authorized all acts necessary and proper for the execution of the powers granted under the Constitution. Hamilton had created the key that would eventually unlock the vault of political power that the Constitution had sought to create. Hamilton's sophistry and cunning would be used to turn the original intention of a constitution to preserve the sovereign states' reserved rights and enforce the limited exercise of Federal powers into a document that would allow for any act that Federal authorities felt was necessary and proper for the functioning of the national government.

Those who supported the Federal Banking Bill in Congress did not have enough votes to pass their legislation. They looked to the president for his support. The president had to choose between two radically different theories—Hamilton's loose construction, which would allow the Federal government to establish the Bank of the United States, or Jefferson's strict construction, which would not allow the Federal government to act without specific constitutional authority. At this most constitutionally significant moment Washington did something so typical of politicians but so untypical of what we have been taught to expect from former General and then President Washington. He made a deal with those in Congress who supported Hamilton's view that in exchange for his support for their bill they would support legislation to move the Federal capital to an area between Maryland and Virginia— an area in which Washington held large tracts of land and of course from which he stood to make a significant profit. And so political maneuvering at the highest levels gave America a loose construction of the Constitution and an open invitation to power-hungry Federal politicians to abuse the grant of power given to the Federal government by the sovereign states.

The Federal Government Sues a Sovereign State (1793)

One of the basic principles of political sovereignty is that the sovereign cannot be compelled into court—the sovereign cannot be sued. During the debate over ratification anti-Federalists warned Americans that the Federal courts proposed in the Constitution would have the power to compel a sovereign state to submit to the court's jurisdiction—a blatant and unacceptable violation of the principle of sovereignty. Alexander Hamilton answered this claim by assuring the anti-Federalists, "I hope that no gentleman will think that a State will be called at the bar of the Federal court... It is not rational to suppose that the sovereign power should be dragged before a court."[5] Despite the plain language of this Federalist promise in 1793, four short years after the ratification of the Constitution, the sovereign state of Georgia was called to defend itself before the Federal court! The legislature of Georgia was so enraged that it passed a resolution declaring that any Federal official who attempted to enforce the Federal court order would be "hung by the neck without benefit of clergy."[6] What do you think the reaction would have been had the same Federal court ordered the sovereign state of Georgia in 1793 to remove all religious symbols from public property or to ban prayer and Bible reading at state events?

The audacity of this Federal power grab served as a warning to those who feared the day when the Federal government would become captive to those who did not share the interests of "we the people" within the sovereign states. This Federal power grab resulted in the rapid proposal and passage of the Eleventh Amendment to the Constitution. This amendment followed

---

5. Alexander Hamilton, as cited in, Kennedy and Kennedy, *Why Not Freedom!*, p. 37.
6. Kennedy and Kennedy, *Was Jefferson Davis Right?*, p. 234.

the spirit of Hamilton's (insincere?) promise by declaring: "The Judicial power of the United States shall not be construed to extend to any suit...against one of the United States..." Notice how the framers of this amendment described the sovereign state as "one" of the United States. They held the correct view that the United States, plural, was composed of distinct and sovereign states—therefore the term used by early constitutional scholars, republic of republics.[7] Unfortunately this view was not held by the Federalists and their philosophical descendants who continued their struggle to establish a strong, centralized, supreme Federal government.

Federal Government Violates Freedom of Speech and Press (1798)

In 1798 the Federal Congress passed the Alien and Sedition Act.[8] The act prohibited public statements in opposition to Federal policies either verbally or written. Numerous citizens including newspaper editors were sent to jail by Federal courts for simply exercising their right of free speech by making critical remarks about the Federal government—a plain violation of the Bill of Rights! To counter this situation Thomas Jefferson and James Madison authored the Kentucky and Virginia Resolutions of 1798. These resolutions were passed by the legislatures of both states. These resolves became the standard for those advocating in favor of limited federalism and State's Rights. The resolves declared that the sovereign states did not establish the Federal government as their superior and that the states had reserved the right to use whatever methods necessary to protect their citizens from an abusive Federal government.[9] As early as 1798, less than a decade after the ratification of the Constitution, two sovereign states and two of the founding fathers were forced to remind those in control of the Federal government that the states, not

---

7. In the *Federalist Papers, Number 32*, the term "partial union," is used and in *Numbers 51* and *62* the phrase "compound republic of America" is used—thus the descriptive term republic (singular) of republics (plural).

8. Space prohibits a full discussion of the Alien and Sedition Act of 1798—for more details see Kennedy and Kennedy, *Was Jefferson Davis Right?*, pp. 88, 178, 234, and 281.

9. Kennedy and Kennedy, *Was Jefferson Davis Right?*, p. 281.

the Federal government, were the final authority as it relates to the liberty of their citizens.

Tariff of Abominations—Taxes, Taxes, Taxes (1826)

In 1826 the Federal Congress passed a protective tariff that was much higher than anything necessary to fund the Federal government. This was in the days before the Federal income tax. The primary means for collecting Federal revenues was via import duties or tariffs. The protective tariff was pushed through Congress in order to force agricultural states to purchase goods manufactured in the North. By this time the commercial interests of the Northern states had become a majority in the Federal Congress. The agricultural states had to purchase manufactured products either from the North or from England or other foreign nations. The tariff imposed on foreign goods drove the price of foreign goods up above the price of Northern goods. "We the people" of the agricultural states were forced to pay a higher price; Northern manufacturers eliminated competition, which allowed them to charge a higher price; and the Federal government gained a windfall profit in "taxes" paid by "we the people" of the agricultural states. To make matters worse, the increased Federal revenues were then used to fund "internal improvements" that benefited primarily the commercial interests of the Northern states. This is why the protective tariff was called the Tariff of Abominations by the agricultural states—primarily Southern states. The sovereign state of South Carolina nullified the tariff and threatened to secede if the Federal government tried to enforce the tariff in South Carolina. By the early 1850s 75 percent of all Federal revenues were extorted via this method from six southern states. According to popular history, in 1861 when Confederate General P. G. T. Beauregard ordered the firing on Fort Sumter in Charleston, South Carolina, the first cannon shot was aimed at the Customs House in the fort that had been used to collect Federal tariffs!

Too often Americans look at their history as if everything worked out for the good of "we the people." This is not necessarily true. Very often, as happens in most political situations, a small cabal of well-organized "special interest" groups will capture control of government and use the police power of government to force "we the people" to accept political and social conditions that eventually work to the disadvantage of those who are not a part of the ruling elite. From the very beginning of the country there have been forces that have wanted to create a strong, centralized, and supreme Federal government and use it to benefit their special interests—even though such benefits worked to the detriment of "we the people." Thomas Jefferson and James Madison knew this would happen because they understood the fallen nature of man—they knew that "we the people" had not found "angels" to rule over us! As Americans know only too well today—the secular humanist ruling elite are not angels!

18

Red States Versus Blue States— America's Great Divide

"Religion should make people feel good, not bad."
National Secular Humanist Talk Show Host

"The mark of a good pastor is that he is always ready to comfort the afflicted and to afflict the comfortable."
Traditional Southern Baptist Truism

Secular humanist propagandists in the liberal media and academia are quick to label moral Americans as "divisive" and lament that if Americans holding traditional conservative, moral values would relent in our allegiance to such outmoded ideas and doctrines, then we could all "just get along." Their goal is not social civility, but an attempt to make sure that "we the people" who hold traditional Christian moral values remain unequally yoked with unbelievers— therefore assuring the political dominance of evil in America. Moral Americans must always keep in mind God's command to be separate—in order for our lives to serve as a sharp contrast to life in the immoral secular humanist world. The division in modern America is not the result of our adherence to traditional Christian morality, but to the successful efforts of the politically active secular humanists to divide America into two mutually antagonistic social camps— those holding traditional moral values and who pay America's tax burden (the forgotten man), and those who hold anti-Christian, secular humanist values and gain more from government than they pay in taxes. America's political division, between Republicans and Democrats, is unique in that it does *not* represent a divide— both parties represent their respective part of an established group (ruling elite), while neither party represents the cares, concerns, and interests of the forgotten man. In actuality America's current political system composed of Republicans and Democrats—who make up America's ruling elite—is not a divide at all!

149

Modern America—A House Divided

America's current political system divides the ruling elite into two groups. In this distorted American system one side wins and the other side loses. The winner spends four to eight years repaying political debts to those who funded their successful campaign and extracting revenge from the loser as payback for the previous four to eight years of political loss suffered while the adversary held political power. In four to eight years the public tires of the antics of the victor and hands the reins of power over to the former vanquished, and the cycle repeats. The end result is that the power elite in Washington retain their high position in the political system but take turns holding the reins of power.

While this political circus is taking place the forgotten man, the law-abiding, taxpaying, moral American, is forced to endure more government, more taxes, and an expanding, anti-Christian, secular humanist political nation regardless of which side won the last election. For the power elite each election is a win-win (of course the actual winner gets more of the spoils of victory, but the loser retains a powerful political position and merely waits for his next turn at power), but for the forgotten man each election is a lose-lose. The forgotten man appears to lose less when "conservatives" win, but he loses nonetheless because conservatives generally expand government though at a slower rate than liberals. Unfortunately for the forgotten man, conservatives never reclaim liberty by reversing policies that tend to promote moral decay in society or return taxes that were stolen from the forgotten man by prior liberal regimes.[1] The end result is more power, privilege, and wealth for the ruling elite and those with close relations to the ruling elite, while the forgotten man, who has no real political power, pays the cost both financially and morally and is simply disregarded out there in "fly-over" country.

"Fly-over" country is a derogatory term used by the ruling elite to describe the unimportant land and people outside of Hollywood, New York, and Washington, D.C. It is used in the same manner that secular humanist news media used "tea bagging" (a term used to

1. James Ronald Kennedy, *Reclaiming Liberty* (Gretna, LA: Pelican Publishing Company, 2005), pp. 15-43.

describe certain acts in pornographic films) to mock productive citizens who engaged in Tea Bag protests against big government spending in 2009. Both terms demonstrate their utter disdain and contempt for moral Americans—thus God's injunction to "Be ye not unequally yoked together with unbelievers."

America's current cultural divide is not between Democrats and Republicans, nor is it between liberals and conservatives. Both of these groups represent their distinct segment of America's political ruling elite. When viewed from a political point of view, America's great divide is between those who believe in *political* slavery and those who believe in *individual* liberty. When viewed culturally, this great divide is between those who support a secular humanist social agenda and those who hold firm to the faith of our fathers and believe in moral principles based on traditional Christian values. Yes, secular humanists and most conservatives believe in *political* slavery! The now defunct and falsified system of communism is an example of the most extreme form of political slavery. Socialism, nominal socialism, and contemporary liberalism are to a lesser degree also forms of *political* slavery. Chattel slavery as practiced in America until the passage of the Thirteenth Amendment in 1866 was the complete denial of the first principle of good government— the principle of self-ownership. It is only slightly different from modern-day political slavery!

Under socialism, liberal social welfare, and conservative corporate welfare,[2] the principle of self-ownership is not completely denied but merely encumbered. The average American taxpayer must labor for his master (Uncle Sam) from January through April or May before he is allowed to keep the fruit of his labor for himself—it takes on average four to five months worth of labor for the typical American

---

2. Corporatism or corporate welfare is a key factor in fascist states. In America, President Dwight David Eisenhower referred to it as the "military-industrial complex." Republicans tend to favor corporatism more than Democrats, while Democrats tend to favor social welfare more than Republicans. Neither is exclusively wedded to one or the other. Both Democrats and Republicans use both corporate and social welfare, but they tend to consistently favor one over the other. For the forgotten man it makes little difference—he pays regardless, and gets little if any benefit.

to earn enough money to pay the taxes "his" government extorts from him each year! But this is only part of the sad story of parasitic exploitation the ruling elite foist upon the forgotten man. Four to five months of forced labor for government accounts for only direct taxes. It does not take into account the cost borne by the forgotten man as a consumer for innumerable unfunded Federal mandates; the cost the forgotten man pays for "market adjustments" caused by the Federal Reserve pumping unsound money into the economy; or the cost borne for inflation—an indirect tax used by government to finance government programs. The total cost of direct taxes levied by Federal, state, and local governments; plus the cost of numerous "market adjustments"; plus the cost of unfunded Federal mandates; plus the cost of inflation, would most likely exceed six months of the forgotten man's labor! Not only is this a drain on the individual's ability to take care of himself and his family, but collectively it is a drain on social wealth. This is due to the fact that money parasitically extorted by the ruling elite is not used to increase social wealth, but it is used to increase the wealth of the ruling elite and those with close connections with the ruling elite—special interests, contractors for government jobs, big banks and other financial interests. Had this money been left in the hands of the productive people who had honestly earned it, the money would have been put to productive use creating savings and real sustainable jobs and products demanded by consumers. This is the way the free market increases social wealth— which is radically different from wealth redistribution practiced by America's ruling elite.

The use of the force of government, actual or implied, is what nineteenth-century American political writers referred to as civil slavery. In reality it is not that much different from the task system of chattel slavery used by some slave owners in the antebellum South. Under the task system, the slave was bound to labor for a given number of days each week, and during those days all of the slave's productive labor would go to his master. After the slave had worked the required number of days for his master, the slave was "free" to keep everything he earned the rest of the week. In modern America the forgotten man labors the required numbers of months for his slave master, Uncle Sam, and then the remaining months he is "free" to labor in order to gain sustenance for himself and his family! Uncle Sam is a "good" master in that he takes the money away from his slaves on the easy-payment plan, just a little at a time over the entire year instead of all at once—this keeps slaves docile and lowers the possibility of a massive slave revolt.

Any political leader—whether Democrat or Republican, liberal or conservative—all politicians in America's current political system are to one degree or another promoting a system of tax-and-spend big government. Such a system will ultimately result not only in the forgotten man's current partial impoverishment and enslavement, but eventually the forgotten man's total impoverishment and enslavement. "We the people" must never forget that in order to be free the self-owning individual's property rights must be secure— not only from social criminals, but also from parasitic political criminals whose crimes benefit the ruling elite and those with close connections to the ruling elite. When government extorts the major portion of an individual's private property, even in the name of socially good projects, the individual is no longer free but is enslaved to his masters in government. Enslavement can take many forms including enslavement to the government. In the modern world, big governments are the largest purveyors of slavery. Any act of government that encumbers man's ability to freely use his private property or that, without his consent, deprives man of all or a portion of the fruit of his labor is an act of enslavement. The mere fact that the enslaving government is sanctified by a majority vote obtained in the democratic process in no way lessens the act of enslavement.

Some would argue that "conservatives" do not believe in social slavery because "conservatives" believe in limited government. The problem with this argument is that every time a "conservative" politician is elected to national office he begins to act like a liberal! He begins to set "earmarks" on legislation allegedly to benefit his constituency back home. But all too often these earmarks and other pork-barrel legislation merely benefit the politician's re-election. And by taking part in the earmarking of legislation the "conservative" has maneuvered himself into a position from which it is impossible for elected conservatives to launch an effect attack on liberal "earmarking" and other liberal pork-barrel spending schemes. By this manner "conservatives" inevitably allow themselves to be co-opted into the American political system of tax and spend, "the public be damned." In reality the conservative politician's hyped belief in limited government is merely political verbal fodder used to feed the human sheep back home so "we the people" will cast our votes for the "most conservative" candidate. In reality this "most conservative" candidate is just another member of the ruling elite whose main interest is not in reducing the weight of government borne by the forgotten man, but in securing the national political *status quo* so the politician's powers, perks, and privileges remain safe for another election cycle.

Religious Divide—Bible Belt States Are Red, Un-churched States Are Blue

A recent survey released by Gallup[3] assessed the importance of religion in each of the states in the United States. The data was collected during 2008. The reality demonstrated by this poll should shock moral Americans and cause them to understand why "we the people" of the states who want to live in a moral society must act, and act now! This poll demonstrated the fact that this is not a country that follows its motto of "In God we trust." In reality this is a country divided along lines of fervent faith and secular humanist attitudes. The states in which the highest percentage of the population responded that religion was important in their daily lives were all to be found in the South. The states in which the lowest percentage of the population responded that religion was important in their daily lives were found to be in New England, plus a few states in the West—Oregon, Washington, Nevada, and Alaska. A map of these states demonstrating those that scored as most religious looks almost identical to a map of the traditional "Bible Belt" states. The important thing to note is that for political purposes those states in the "least religious" states compose America's numerical majority, while those states in the most religious states compose America's moral minority. In America's contemporary political system the numerical majority imposes its will upon the numerical minority— the secular humanists control, and moral Americans must obey! This leaves moral Americans facing the ancient question, "Shall we obey man or God?"

The 2008 Gallup poll is similar to a Pew Research poll conducted

3. www.gallup.com/poll/114022/State-States-Importance-Religiion.aspx?version=print (accessed 3/21/09).

in 2006 (discussed in Addendum II of this book). The Pew Research demonstrated that the people in the Southern states gave a higher percentage of their income to charity, while the people of the New England states gave the smallest percentage of income to charity. This is even more startling when considering the fact that the Southern states are, and have been since 1865, the poorest states of the Union, while the New England states are the richest states in the Union! The people of the state of Mississippi, the poorest state in the Union, gave the highest percentage of their income to charity; whereas the people of the state of Massachusetts, one of the richest states in the Union, gave the lowest percentage of their income to charity. If ever there was a national example of the selfless piety of the widow's mite and the selfish pride of the rich ruler, it is here in the actions and inactions of the people of the religious South and the secular humanist New England.

People with strong Christian faith accept their duty to follow the Lord's command to "Do unto others as you would have them do unto you." Even Christians with relatively limited financial resources will find a way to help those in distress—it takes God to change a sinful and selfish heart into a loving and giving heart. God-government can force people to "give" to a political cause, that always benefits the ruling elite, but it cannot change the innate tendency of man's heart—it takes God to get the "gutter out of the man." In a moral community charity is not something done under compulsion or threat of force but out of a sense of duty to God and man. A moral community does not need the force of government to take care of the deserving needy; whereas a secular humanist community not only needs government, it actively encourages the expansion of government. There is a reason why secular humanists encourage the expansion of government. They do it because they know that a secular humanist society cannot exist without the all-powerful, compelling force of government.

Secular humanists need government in order to foist their views upon moral people who do not share their immoral worldview. This is demonstrated not only by the two polls just discussed, but also by a map showing the Red States and Blue States in the presidential elections of 2004 and 2008. These national elections demonstrate why "we the people" who compose the moral majority within our states must act to reclaim the right to control our states. In 2008 the conservative candidate for president was far less "conservative" than most moral conservatives wanted him to be.[4] Yet, still the religious and charitable states, with two exceptions, voted for the conservative candidate—becoming once again Red States. The less religious and non-charitable states voted for the nominal socialist (extreme liberal) candidate—becoming once again Blue States. This great Red States-Blue States divide is based on moral values. Secular humanists have reached the tipping point where their Federal government has enough voters on its welfare and entitlement rolls that it can control the Federal government through the electoral process. With the backing of Federal power, secular humanists can now move to consolidate their victory by enacting laws, regulations, and taxing policy that will eventually eliminate the moral minority as an effective opponent. This will hold true only as long as "we the people" accept the current perverted version of America's political system. "We the people" can reclaim our liberty—moral communities can be established and protected within our sovereign states—all that is needed is the correct understanding of our founding fathers' original intentions and the will to act.

4. It was evident early in the 2008 Republican primary that the GOP establishment wanted the nominal conservative, John McCain, to be their standard-bearer. This is the same GOP establishment that wanted Bob Dole to face Bill Clinton in the 1996 presidential campaign. The ruling elite always select candidates based on membership in the elite, not on principles they espouse.

19

Sovereign States: The Prerequisite for Creating Moral Communities

"Whensoever the general government assumes undelegated powers, its acts are un-authoritative, void, and of no force."
Kentucky Resolution 1798 (Thomas Jefferson)

"In cases of a deliberate, palpable, and dangerous exercise of other powers not granted by the said compact, the States, who are parties thereto, have a right, and are in duty bound, to interpose for arresting the progress of the evil."
Virginia Resolution 1798 (James Madison)

Utopian dreamers and socialist visionaries in early America initiated separatist movements in which they would move away from general society and live in a communal society.[1] A list of the various "separatist" movements in contemporary America would include divergent groups such as white and black supremacists who also promote the establishment of communities to isolate themselves from society. All such separatist movements, both past and present, are based on the principle that "true" believers must physically separate themselves from society and create a more perfect world within the physical boundaries of their particular community.

Spiritual Separation

God's commandment to "Be ye separate" does not contemplate physical separation. It contemplates separation from evil, but such separation does not require that moral people live in isolation, physically separated from the world. God's commandment to be separate requires spiritual separation from an ungodly world. The

---

1. Walter D. Kennedy and Al Benson, Jr., *Red Republicans and Lincoln's Marxists* (Lincoln, NE: iUniverse Press, 2007), pp. 7-26.

issue contemporary moral Americans face is how to live a moral life, pass moral values on to children, and provide an environment in which moral attitudes will be the norm and not treated as abnormal, deviant, and politically incorrect. The issue is reduced to the question "How can moral people maintain moral standards in a nation ruled and influenced by secular humanists who use government to promote and enforce their anti-Christian worldview?"

America's contemporary social values are established by Hollywood, the secular humanist news media, a secular humanist education system, and corrupt business leaders and politicians more so than by the teachings of biblical morality. America's moral code is no longer established by a "moral majority." The hippies of the late 1960s whose moral code was "If it feels good—do it" have given America a whole generation of leaders whose moral code is "If it's good for me, and I think I can get away with it—do it." This immoral and hedonistic secular humanist code has brought America's morals down to the level of the brothel; it has reduced our language to the level of expletives that would embarrass sailors of prior generations; it has given us cities where the probability of dying as a result of violence is greater than that of a soldier serving in Iraq at the height of the war; and it has produced a nation in which vast parts of the population have a parasitic entitlement mentality in which they expect and demand that government provide them their share of other people's money. Yet, regardless of the current sad state of affairs, Americans can take heart in the knowledge that God is still on His throne and America's founding fathers left "we the people" a means to establish and protect moral communities!

Political Separation

Christians must understand that the key to establishing and protecting moral communities in modern America is political separation—not physical separation. Political separation means that within our sovereign communities "we the people" will exercise the ultimate authority relative to political decisions impacting our communities. The corporate representative of the sovereign community is the sovereign state. For example, when the Federal government ordered the removal of the Ten Commandments from a courthouse in the state of Alabama, instead of meekly submitting to the unconstitutional Federal order the sovereign state of Alabama would have, under our plan, the ability to exercise, on behalf of the sovereign community, its inalienable right to defend the reserved rights of "we the people" by nullifying the Federal order. Of course in America's contemporary governmental system this could not be done, but "we the people" have, with God's help, the power to change the system and reclaim our lost rights.

The political solution being proposed is not revolutionary—indeed it is simply a return to the system of government that follows the letter and spirit of the founding fathers' original intentions for American government. When men such as Thomas Jefferson and James Madison were faced with an abusive Federal government that violated its constitutional authority by oppressing the rights of free speech, they did not meekly submit! They announced to the world in the Kentucky and Virginia Resolves of 1798 that the sovereign state would not allow its agent, the Federal government, to violate the rights of "we the people" within their states.

During the late 1850s the question of slavery agitated the states. Even though the Constitution required in Article IV, Section 2, that states return fugitive slaves, many Northern states felt this to be a violation of their moral code. When faced with the question of whether they should obey man's law or what they felt to be God's law, "we the people" of those states answered by ignoring the offending portion of the Constitution, which amounted to a *de facto* nullification of a portion of the U.S. Constitution.

Suppose a new Federal law or Federal court order were issued declaring that any speech describing an individual's choice of sexual orientation or lifestyle as evil would be a Federal hate crime and subject to the jurisdiction of the Federal Office of Civil Rights. Under such a law Christians would be compelled to remove certain sections of the Bible and refrain from preaching sermons that declare or imply that such lifestyles are contrary to God's expressed will. Even if Christians were willing to do so (God forbid!), what would happen when the Federal government next ordered churches to take affirmative action to remove past discrimination by teaching alternative lifestyles in Sunday Schools? What recourse would "we the people" who hold biblical moral values have against an all-powerful Federal government? The sad reality would be that in America's contemporary political system there would exist no effective political alternative! Oh yes, we could petition, demonstrate, hold meeting, and when such petty activities and complaints had exhausted "we the people," the only alternative left would be to meekly obey. The ruling elite allowed us the "freedom" to complain, and now it is time for "we the people" to obey our masters.

Such an extreme scenario may be unlikely to occur,[2] but it does make clear just how vulnerable "we the people" are since we can no longer rely on the sovereign state to protect our rights and liberties from an abusive Federal government. It also demonstrates the way that state sovereignty could be used to peacefully resolve conflicts about extremely divergent and emotionally sensitive social issues. Remember that Christians, unlike our secular humanist opponents, must follow the Lord's command to "Do unto others as you would have them do unto you"; therefore, Christians must not use force to compel compliance with our worldview. Secular humanists, on the other hand, cannot sustain their worldview without relying on the use of *illegitimate* government force. If the moral community within a sovereign state decides to nullify a particular Federal action, the act of nullification in no way alters the Federal act for those residing in states with a secular humanist majority and who favor such Federal acts. Under this scenario life goes on throughout the United States without the threat of violence, and the rights of the numerical minority are respected within the confines of their particular state. The secular humanists can have their Federal law, it will be enforced within those states that agree with it; and the moral minority (nationally) who represent a majority within their state are not forced to support a law that violates their moral code. A major benefit of state sovereignty, and the right of nullification that naturally flows from it, is that because the majority knows that laws oppressive of the rights of the minority will be nullified—there is less motive to enact such laws. Nullification encourages political

2. Such a scenario may not be as unlikely as some may think—it sounds like something a Federal official like Rep. Barney Frank, a liberal Congressmen, would sponsor. It would certainly receive great support from secular humanists throughout the nation.

civility as it relates to the relations between the numerical majority and the numerical minority.

Moral People First, Then Moral Political Action

As already noted, God's commandment to be separate is first a spiritual command. Before a people can establish a moral community a majority must first be moral individuals—not just "good" people. Many secular humanists are "good" people, but as Christians understand, it takes more than being "good" by worldly standards to qualify as being a biblical moral person. Personal redemption is the work of God and His Church. It requires a firm foundation in Holy Scriptures and faith in the redemptive work of Jesus Christ. This is an entirely personal and private matter to be worked out by each individual. It is not something to be poured in from the top by government—this holds true regardless of whether the government is controlled by secular humanists or Christians.

There is a danger though in Christians becoming moral egotists—where we think that if others do not believe exactly as we do, they are not moral people. Christians are warned against such judgments. A moral community does not require a religious litmus test—how often people attend church, how much they give to the church, or outward manifestations of religion. Not everyone within the sovereign community will hold the same religious views and values. There will be great diversity of and tolerance for differing beliefs and practices. Not everyone will be a Christian—some will hold entirely different religious views. A moral community does not use the force of government to compel people to accept a particular worldview—even if such acts of compulsion could easily be sanctified by a majority vote. Christians should leave acts of governmental force, threats, and coercion to the secular humanists.

Political Action to Reclaim Liberty

How do "we the people" create moral communities in an immoral nation? One thing certain is that America's ruling elite—liberals, nominal socialists, and establishment conservative Republicans—will not take a friendly view of any effort to limit their perks, privileges, and power. The reason that secular humanists, liberals, and nominal socialists will resist is obvious—their worldview cannot exist absent the oppressive force of government. But why will "conservative" Republicans resist this effort? The answer is simple—just like secular humanists and liberals, establishment Republicans have a vested interest in maintaining the *status quo*.

For generations America's ruling elite have used the power of government to extort money from the forgotten man and use it for political purposes that always benefit the ruling elite. And never overlook the fact that establishment Republicans are an integral part of America's ruling elite. The habit of oppressive government is so ingrained in their psychological makeup that to the ruling elite their actions are not oppressive but a natural outgrowth of their rights as elected officials. They have a mental picture of themselves as being "public servants," and therefore anything they do in the name of the public is legitimate. When the ruling elite are informed of the forgotten man's complaint, they immediately assume it is just the aberrant moaning of an insignificant, unpatriotic, and unlearned individual. They usually handle such complaints by merely ignoring them, and in most cases those complaining soon realize the improbability of any effectual changes, tire of the exhausting efforts needed to "fight city hall," and eventually give up. If ignoring the forgotten man's complaints does not work, then the ruling elite can rely on their friends in the secular humanist media and universities to demonize the complaining forgotten man. For example, if a taxpayer complains about the cost of social welfare, he can usually be silenced by having the secular humanist press slander the forgotten man by calling him a racist. The point is that anyone who intends to do the Lord's work can expect a fight with the devil. This is as true for political issues as it is for spiritual issues. The need to control our communities, to create a moral environment in which to raise our children, is certainly the Lord's work, but it will not be accomplished without a struggle.

Electing Statesmen

In chapter 11 we discussed the difference between statesmen and politicians. It will not be an easy task to find candidates who are true statesmen, and even more difficult to elect them. But political power is the only way we can create a moral community—a community protected by the authority of the sovereign state. When politicians win elective office they have three main objectives to accomplish prior to the next election: (1) maintain the *status quo*, which provides them the perks, privileges, and power they enjoy; (2) do those things necessary to repay those who provided the financial resources needed to capture the public office, and (3) do those things necessary to assure their re-election. Contrast the politician's main objectives with the main objective facing a statesman when he gains elective office—do those things necessary to reduce the size and scope of government. The politician steals OPM and gives it to those closely associated with the politician and makes numerous public appearances in which he is able to demonstrate how effective he is in "bringing his constituents their share of the government's pie back to his district." In Congress this is done via earmarks that result in "bridges to nowhere." A statesman on the other hand can only work to reduce the burden of government borne by the taxpayer. There is little opportunity for public celebration when a useless government project is blocked or eliminated. Because the news media is dominated by secular humanists, liberals, and nominal socialists, they miss no opportunity to tell the public just how ineffective the statesman is and how he is failing his constituents. Of course their hidden agenda is to "demonize" the statesman so he will be easy to defeat at the next election by a business-as-usual politician. Under these circumstances—no one in his right mind would be so foolish as to run for office without the protection of the ruling elite. What we need are men and women who are foolish by the world's standard and who have faith that the foolish things of God will confound the wisdom of the wise.

New Political Methods for a New Political System

It is impossible to establish moral communities in a country ruled by secular humanists, liberals, nominal socialists, and business-as-usual conservatives using traditional political methods. The results from past political efforts should demonstrate to even a casual observer that old ways are failed ways. If "we the people" keep doing the same things we have always done, we will always end up with the same sad results! Look around at America's current moral values and see the result of electing "good" family-values conservatives. Even "good" conservatives once elected must work within the current political system; a system that is designed to favor the ruling elite; a system in which elected officials have a vested interest in maintaining the *status quo*; a corrupt and corrupting system that quickly converts "good" conservatives into loyal Democrats or Republicans. Our efforts must be directed toward replacing not fixing a broken political system. From this day forward elections are not about winning office but about reclaiming liberty!

Prior to an election in which one of our statesmen seeks a public office "we the people" who want to establish a political system that will allow for the creation of moral communities must spend a great deal of time, effort, and resources convincing our neighbors of the importance of our movement. Every Christian residing within the electoral district being contested must be informed of this movement prior to the election—prior to our statesman announcing his candidacy. This will require a great deal of effort to educate our fellow citizens—men and women who have become so conditioned to living in an immoral country that they no longer have hope of a better country. It is our duty to give hope back to God's people—one person at a time.

Political campaigns that occur after our initial education efforts will be used as another method to educate the public. The primary purpose is *not* to win elections but to make our position known to the people within our communities. Political campaigns that are well organized and given adequate funding by supporters of our cause will be a success regardless of the final vote tally. Success is measured by the ability to speak publicly about our cause and to win new supporters. Winning elections will be the natural and eventual outgrowth of these educational efforts. But always keep in mind that winning is not the first purpose of the political campaign— educating the public about the possibility of reclaiming lost rights and the possibility of establishing a moral community within our state is the primary purpose. Those who are elected on our ticket will use the "bully pulpit" of their office to continue the education efforts and encourage people in other communities to join the movement. Eventually every Christian in the United States will know about our goal to establish a new political system—one that will remove forever the ability of the immoral numerical majority to foist their immoral values upon our moral communities.

Constitutional Amendment to Reclaim State's Rights
The only way to make an effective and permanent change in

America's current political system is to amend the Constitution in order to restore the ability of "we the people" acting through our sovereign state to nullify oppressive acts of the Federal government. This reserved right was never legally removed, but the current political system acts as though this right never existed. Most Americans are shocked when they learn that anyone would even suggest such a right exists—this is clear proof of just how utterly dominated and miseducated (propagandized) the once proud and free people of America have become. It also demonstrates why education of "we the people" is such an important factor in the success of this movement.

A complete description and discussion of the required constitutional amendment can be found in other books[3] and will not be repeated here. The demand for a radical change in the current political system must come from the grassroots—it cannot be imposed from the top because those at the top (the ruling elite) have a vested interest in maintaining the *status quo*. We must elect enough of "our" statesmen to Congress to introduce (but not necessarily pass) the amendment. After it is introduced in Congress "we the people" within every congressional district must be organized to the point that we can force members of Congress (representatives and senators) to support the proposed amendment; if they refuse, we must be able to replace them at the next election. The proposed constitutional amendment must receive at least a two-thirds vote in both houses of Congress; then it will be submitted to the states for ratification. Three-fourths of the state legislatures must approve the proposed amendment in order for it to be ratified as an amendment to the Constitution. The process is difficult but not impossible. To be successful only three things are required: (1) God's blessing; (2) Christians who are educated about the moral justification for this movement; and (3) an organized and dedicated group of moral, law-abiding, taxpaying citizens.

3. See James Ronald Kennedy and Walter Donald Kennedy, *Why Not Freedom!* (Gretna, LA: Pelican Publishing Company, 1994), pp. 289-97, or James Ronald Kennedy, *Reclaiming Liberty* (Gretna, LA: Pelican Publishing Company, 2005), pp. 76, 79, 258.

Once this movement accomplishes its goal of securing true State's Rights, then the rights and liberties of the numerical moral minority will no longer be at risk every four years or each time secular humanists attempt to put one of their judges on the U.S. Supreme Court. Nor will "we the people" of the sovereign community be at risk of having a Congress dominated by secular humanists and business-as-usual conservatives who enact laws or raise taxes in violation of our moral code. But the great question at this point is "Can it be done?"

20

God and Gideon—Can We Do It?

"With God all things are possible."

Matthew 19:26

"One person who believes is worth more than a hundred who are merely interested."

Anonymous

The major question troubling many readers at this point is "Can it be done?" Can "we the people" reclaim the right to control the moral values within our communities? Even though it would be great, for one of many possible examples, to be able to have our state protect the life of an unborn child by setting the point at which life begins—can it be done? The point is that moral Americans are nationally a numerical minority, and the secular humanists who represent the national numerical majority will not voluntarily relent in their oppressive use of Federal power to impose their pagan worldview upon Christians. Can "we the people" reclaim our lost rights? The answer to this question is "No, we cannot!" By ourselves we cannot accomplish this task, but with God's help all things are possible.

With God's help and three hundred dedicated men Gideon defeated the numerically superior host of Midian. The Bible has numerous examples of how the "foolishness" of God is used to confound the wisdom of the wise. The main obstacle facing moral Americans is the fact that we have become a very impatient people. We lead lives full of "road rage." Like children, we demand instant gratification of all our desires. We tend to expect things to happen quickly on our timetable instead of faithfully enduring, waiting upon the Lord, and having faith that God's time line is not the same as ours, but that in the end, His ways will be victorious for we are assured that His providence is sure. The essential element of faith is the ability to believe even though there is no physical evidence to support that faith. A great deal of effort, prayer, and sacrifice will be made long before our first victory at the ballot box. The first election victory will be followed by many more months and years of effort, prayer, and sacrifice. This effort will require patience and persistence over a long period of time—years, not just months. We must have faith that this struggle to establish moral communities within the United States is something that God wants Christians to do. Faith is required in order to believe in the eventual success of our movement. Faith in the eventual outcome is required to maintain this effort because we will be doing battle with the forces of evil with which there is no compromise. Their desire is to destroy Christian morality and to use the force of government to replace Christian values with their secular humanist values. What was required for Gideon's victory over a numerically superior army? Faith in God, faith in the righteousness of the cause for which he and his men were fighting, and willingness to endure as long as necessary the hardships of the struggle against God's enemies. The same is true for moral Americans. God plus one is a majority regardless of what the wisdom of the wise may claim!

It is important to note that Gideon was able to defeat the numerically superior enemy with a small dedicated band of followers. The same holds true for our cause. A small number of dedicated individuals in each local community can educate their community about this cause. As more people are added to the group of local supporters the possibility of launching a successful political campaign increases. Each political campaign is another opportunity to educate the voting public. Eventually, as more and more people become supporters of our cause, our candidates (statesmen, not politicians) will begin winning public office, and our statesmen will use the "bully pulpit" of their elective office to educate people throughout the state. We must start at the local level and build a network of supporters, because eventually we will need their support to convince members of Congress to support our constitutional amendment. If they refuse, then we will need supporters to help us remove those irreconcilable politicians and replace them with true statesmen.

As was noted earlier, the ruling elite will first ignore our movement and hope that "we the people" will tire of fighting the politically correct establishment. Once we begin winning elective office, the ruling elite will switch from ignoring our movement to unleashing their politically correct attack dogs in academia and their supporters in the leftist news media. The viciousness of their attacks must not be underrated. They will use every dirty trick in the book in an effort to defeat this movement. Why? Because the ruling elite know that once our cause becomes known in other states their tenure in power will be over forever! For generations they, both Democrats and Republicans, have enjoyed the perks, privileges, and power that attaches to their political positions. The thought of having to surrender their luxurious, parasitic lifestyle and begin to earn an honest living is more than they are willing to tolerate. They will be fighting to maintain the *status quo* that serves them so well, but "we the people" will be fighting to get the ruling elite out of our pockets and off of our backs—we will be fighting to regain our liberty!

Answering Objections
1. "If we cannot win 51 percent of the vote in a presidential election, how can we expect to gain approval of three-fourths of the state legislatures?"

This objection is based on the Red State-Blue State divide in the last several presidential elections. John McCain, who was touted as a conservative, carried twenty-nine states in the 2008 presidential election. If we assume that we could win ratification of a constitutional amendment acknowledging the right of state nullification in each of these states, that would leave us needing only nine more state ratifications. If you look at the twenty-one states that Barack Obama carried, you will find ten states in which (1) the number of evangelicals[1] represents between 22 and 33 percent of the voters, (2) the percentage of gun owners ranges between 21 and 44 percent, and (3) the vote that McCain received was between 40 and 49 percent of the total vote. The possibility of convincing another 2

---

1. www.vaughns-1-pagers.com/politics/red-blue-states-summary.htm (accessed 3/21/2009). Because this data listed only evangelicals it would indicate that the number of practicing Christians would be much larger than the percentage listed for only evangelicals. This would increase the potential support base for ratification in each state.

to 12 percent of the voters in these states to support ratification of a constitutional amendment is very good. In other words, it is not an impossible task as long as we have faith and remain constant in our efforts. Another point is that during the last George W. Bush administration there were many secular humanists who lamented the fact that they were being forced to support Federal policies that were in violation of their principles. We may find that there are many of our opponents who are willing to support our efforts just to avoid a repeat of their experiences as the numerical minority during the Bush years! Another point of encouragement is that a recent study of the importance of religion to the people of the various states demonstrated that there remains a strong religious foundation in all states. Even in Vermont, the state that scored the lowest, almost one half of the population, 42 percent, answered that religion was important to them in their daily life. This poll demonstrated that overall in the United States 65 percent of the population answered that religion was important to them in their daily lives. Unfortunately this does not consistently translate into Americans electing public officials who truly support the rights and values of moral Americans who pay the taxes and obey the law. But it certainly indicates a strong possibility of converting a majority in each state to our cause.

2. "You unjustly refer to all elected officials as being part of the parasitic ruling elite, but I know good and honest men who hold public office."

We are aware of good elected officials holding statewide and local elective office. We know of justices of the peace and district judges who perform their duties in an exemplary manner. We are sure there are others. But the existence of one, two, or even dozens of such elected officeholders does not change the fact that America's current political system has been perverted to serve the ruling elite, those with close connections to the ruling elite, special interest groups that provide funding and votes to re-elect the ruling elite—and all paid for by the forgotten man. We all should be well aware that the current political system tends to corrupt good "family values" conservatives—certainly we do not need to repeat the headlines in the profane media when they celebrate the moral defeat of yet another "conservative," "family values" member of Congress! Even those who go to Washington with the best of intentions often become part of the "Beltway" crowd and eventually end up participating in politics as usual—maintaining the *status quo*. When our movement begins to gain support across the country, it will be interesting to see how many of these "good" politicians come over to our side and help pass our amendment, and how many will give lip service to our efforts but secretively work behind the scene in hopes of defeating us.

3. "There is no way we could ever pass such an amendment—after all, you are talking about changing the very form of America's current government! They are too strong, too entrenched, and have too much political power—we could never overcome such strength!"

There are those of us who remember when the civil rights movement began. Many people felt that it would never succeed, but they were wrong! Not only did black Southerners succeed, but in the process they taught the majority of their white Christian neighbors a lesson about enduring and persisting against great odds, and in the process converted a society from a socially endorsed system of racial segregation to one in which the majority believe in and practice equal respect. If black Christians can make such a dramatic social impact, what makes you think that all Christians could not make an equally important social impact?

Some may also recall that during the 1980s while the Soviet Union was undergoing dramatic change, the small Baltic states began to demand their freedom. They had been under Soviet rule for more than fifty years. In many of the Baltic states there were more Russians living in their country than native peoples. The Russian military had large installations there, and the Communist secret police were actively suppressing dissent. With no friends in the world willing to come to their aid, independence of the Baltic states seemed a lost cause. But their religious faith, their cultural traditions, and their tenacity of spirit eventually won when all three Baltic states seceded from the Soviet Union. Faith and determination will always overcome evil—if we are willing to pay the price.

4. "We should not mix politics and religion. Christians have no business using their faith as an excuse to seek public office."

While we agree that the Church should not be engaged in political contests, it is equally important to remember that Christians have a duty to do those things within their power to influence the creation and maintenance of a society with biblical-based moral values. If Christians do not engage in the political process, they leave non-Christians in charge of the political system. The Roman Catholic Church was a key player in Poland's struggle to throw off Soviet domination. The Church supplied the Polish people spiritual support and succor during a very dangerous period of their history. During the secession struggle in the Baltic states, there was a hill on which the patriots would plant homemade crosses—the Communist authorities would bulldoze the crosses, but the people would slip back and replace them! This act of faith and defiance is an example of how important religion is to a people seeking to regain control of their society. The indispensable role of black churches during the civil rights struggle of the 1950s and 1960s is well known. The Christian faith has an indispensable role to play in the movement to create moral communities. As one of America's founding fathers, John Adams, noted: "Avarice, ambition would break the strongest cords of our Constitution as a whale goes through the net. Our Constitution is made only for a moral and religious people. It is wholly inadequate to the government of any other."[2]

5. "Amending the Constitution is too difficult; don't you think we should spend our time and efforts toward electing good conservatives to Congress?"

There are two major problems with this line of reasoning. First, as recent history has more than adequately demonstrated—no corrective actions occurs even when we have "good" conservatives controlling Congress and occupying the White House![3] Big government is a permanent fixture in America regardless of which political party controls the various departments of the Federal government. Even when Mr. Conservative, Ronald Reagan, was president, the size of the Federal government did not decrease. The

2. As cited by Patrick J. Buchanan, "Systemic Failure," http://www.humanevents. com/article.php?id=31154 (accessed 3/20/2009).

3. For a more detailed explanation see James Ronald Kennedy, "Conservatism: A Century of Failure," in *Regaining Liberty* (Gretna, LA: Pelican Publishing Company, 2005), pp. 15-43.

only thing that was accomplished during the Reagan administration was that the rate of increase in the size of the Federal government was temporarily decreased! In November of 1994 Newt Gingrich's Contract for America produced a Republican majority in the House of Representatives for the first time in decades. It was hailed as the beginning of the end of big government. Some of us who have studied the oppressive nature of the Federal government predicted that the new Republican majority would not reduce the size and scope of the Federal government.[4] It did not take long before the new Republican majority began acting just like the old Democratic majority in that it began to try to buy its re-election by passing pork-barrel programs and various special-interest earmarked legislation. In the end the vaunted Republican "Conservative" Revolution was shown to be nothing more than a weak reflection of its Democratic rival. Thus another lesson to be learned—"we the people" will never win if we rely on electing "good" conservatives.

The second problem with relying on electing good conservatives is that even when they intend to do good the system is designed to work in favor of the power elite to help them maintain their luxurious and parasitic lifestyle. It falls to the forgotten man to pay for the ruling elite's parasitic lifestyle. The original American system of a constitutionally limited republic of republics has been perverted into a system of Federal supremacy in which the two political parties are both dedicated to maintaining the *status quo*. What about the forgotten man? Well, he gets to pay the bill! No, electing business-as-usual conservatives will not solve our problem—we have been trying that prescription to cure our political ills for decades, and it has been a complete failure. Perhaps we should try another remedy before the patient dies!

6. "Your proposal to allow the states to nullify acts of the Federal government would completely weaken if not totally destroy the Federal government! Where would we be without a strong Federal government to protect us?"

4. James Ronald Kennedy and Walter Donald Kennedy, *Why Not Freedom!* (Gretna, LA: Pelican Publishing Company, 1994), pp. 271-72, 277, 311.

"We the people" do not need the help of a large central government to protect us at the local level. We are more than competent to take care of ourselves, especially if the Federal government is prevented from taxing or inflating away the fruit of the workingman's labor. The sad reality is that when it comes to protecting "we the people" in the one area the Federal government is specifically authorized, protecting our borders from invasion, the Federal government is a dismal failure. This is not because the Federal government does not have the authority, power, or resources to protect us, but because the power elite are afraid that if they take strong action it may cause them to lose votes from certain special-interest voting blocs in the next election. The Federal government's role in America has been perverted to the benefit of the ruling elite and the detriment of the forgotten man. Once we remove the ruling elite by returning the United States government to its true role in a constitutionally limited republic of republics, then our security will be assured and the property rights of the forgotten man will be secured as well.

Section IV

Addenda

Addendum I

Katrina: Death by Government
James Ronald Kennedy

If you did not live through it you would not understand! The worst natural disaster in American history was more than a news event for those of us in the middle of it. Prior to Katrina, America's worst natural disaster had resulted in the destruction of approximately 20,000 homes—the destruction of even one home is deplorable in itself but by comparison—Katrina destroyed approximately 200,000 homes and left thousands dead in its wake. In the years following Katrina much has been written, mostly by those observing it from afar. But as one who lived through it; one who has spent much of his life studying and observing the operations of government, I believe the fault for the death and destruction lies not with Mother Nature but with government in general and specifically with the minions of government who placed their faith in "god-government."

A Sick Society is Unprepared for Crisis of Any Kind

There are several basic requirements for a free society to be sustainable. In order for a free community to maintain its existence citizens must possess certain characteristics. One of the first requirements is that a majority of its citizens must be future oriented. To avoid lengthy philosophical verbiage—just think of the ant versus the grasshopper! In a healthy free society people are willing to delay present enjoyment and consumption in favor of working or saving for a better future condition. Another key characteristic is personal responsibility and strict social accountability for personal failure regarding the duty of personal responsibility. Again, avoiding lengthy philosophical verbiage, think of the biblical story of Noah. He took personal responsibility to hear God and to follow God's instructions. In so doing he saved himself and his family. OK, that takes care of personal responsibility, but what, you may ask, about social accountability for personal failure regarding the duty of personal responsibility? Here it becomes a little harsh—especially if you have been spoon-fed by the ACLU and kindred spirits on the Pablum of bleeding-heart liberalism. As the waters rose around Noah's ark, what sounds do you think were heard on the outside? The sounds of thousands of human beings of the grasshopper school of life beating on the walls of the ark and chanting in unison, "Help us, help us, help us," a sound that was slowly silenced by the God-sent rising waters. Don't get me wrong, I am not implying that Katrina or any other natural disaster was sent by God to punish the wicked— other than a few notably recorded cases in the Old Testament. What I am saying is that in our world the tendency of the people in a society to be present oriented, favoring current pleasure and consumption over delayed gratification, will invariably lead to social disaster. This is especially true when that society not only refuses to discourage present thinking, but by its political actions actually encourages present thinking while discouraging future thinking.

While individual responsibility and personal accountability are important in a healthy free society, we must not assume that the individual is an island. A healthy and free society is not a collection of people engaged in living a life of radical individualism—think of individuals living by the creed of "I can do anything as long as it does not directly harm anyone other than me." Certainly the individual is free, but he must exercise his freedom within the voluntary constraints of the family from which he derived his existence and which sustains him in all the joys and turmoil that life brings. Think of the family—in its most economic sense—as a living insurance policy. Like any insurance policy the family is a contract containing rights and duties that both parties must honor. "If it feels good—do it" is the motto of radical individualism, but such thoughts are limited in a healthy free society by a sense of duty to the family—a duty that is voluntarily assumed by cooperative individuals working for their own self-interest while maintaining their duty to the family. For example, prior to the imminent arrival of a hurricane, individuals could spend their time partying, loafing around, or "cruising" the neighborhood looking for moments of criminal opportunity. On the other hand, they could remember their responsibility to the members of their family and start making plans for the family's survival during the impending crisis. Radical individualism encourages individuals to "party on," while the duty of individuals living in a healthy free society encourages individuals to forego personal pleasure in order to secure the safety of the family. Remember, in both cases, radical individualism and individuals in a healthy free society; the individual voluntarily dictates his actions—note the absence of political compulsion.

A healthy free society is a collection of free individuals living within the context of duty owed to the members of the family and a society that encourages and rewards future thinking while allowing individuals who spend an inordinate amount of time in current consumption or present thinking to suffer the personal disaster they bring upon themselves. This does not rule out charity or human compassion—but charity in its classical sense is directed toward those who through no fault of their own find themselves in need. As long as charity is directed as a voluntary activity, then this is fine, but sometimes a harsh distinction must be made. But when government assumes the role of "welfare as a right," then no real distinction can be made, and instead of eliminating need, government subsidizes current need and assures the expansion of need into the future by facilitating mass present thinking on the part of its minions.

What Worked During Katrina—Free Individuals

It is interesting to note that the success stories during Katrina tended to center around free individuals voluntarily working together for their own self-interest and to a lesser extent local governments that were outside of the politically correct corridor known as Orleans Parish. For instance, little has been said about the fact that prior to landfall, southeast Louisiana and the Gulf Coast of Mississippi successfully conducted the largest mass evacuation over the shortest time frame in American history! More than 90% of the population of a major metropolitan center was evacuated—this had never been done—yet it was done, and done with relative efficiency. But that is not the important point. The important point is to note who was responsible for this major evacuation—individuals. The government did not manage the evacuation; the government did not fill up gas tanks, make hotel reservations, contact family members outside the affected area, nor do the thousands of other things necessary for such an event to take place. No, it was individuals thinking ahead who took care of themselves, their families, and their neighbors. Can you even begin to imagine what would have happened had FEMA been responsible for evacuating these people!

Immediately after the storm passed, it was not government (local, state, or Federal) that went door to door checking on friends, neighbors, and perfect strangers. It was not government that brought out their chainsaws and cleared fallen trees from roadways; it was not government that brought in immediate supplies of food, water, and medical aid—no, it was free individuals doing what free individuals in a healthy society always do—voluntarily working together for the good of the community. While President George W. Bush was telling FEMA Director Michael D. Brown, "Brownie, you're doing a heck of a job," I drove through fallen timbers to check on my ninety-year-old mother who lived two hundred miles away from the coast of Mississippi and presumably out of harm's way. This had been the case when Hurricane Camille struck the Mississippi coast in 1968, but not so this time! My twin brother soon had four families living with him, but this is what families do—"Do this for me today because tomorrow I may have to return the favor." The family works like an insurance contract whose currency is love.

While FEMA Director Brown was sending e-mails to his secretary regarding his selection of wardrobe, country people in Louisiana and Mississippi were firing up their tractors and chainsaws to begin the immediate task of restoring communications via the roads and removing trees from homes. While a certain female governor stood around looking for all the world like the proverbial doe in the headlights, church groups were organizing relief supplies and workers to send to the affected areas. But of course government had a role to play—because this disaster presented yet another opportunity for politicians to demonstrate to their minions just how dependent they are on government and why the minions should vote the politicians back into office as soon as possible. But even during such "photo opportunity" moments, government could not function efficiently. I recall the dismay of volunteers who brought their boats to Jefferson Parish to help in the rescue efforts but were prevented from launching their boats because a FEMA official was not satisfied that everyone had appropriate insurance and safety equipment—this while people were literally drowning! In Mississippi, people were without food, water, and ice during the hottest September on record. While the people were suffering, FEMA had supplies stockpiled locally but was refusing to release it because of lack of appropriate paperwork! The local sheriff "took the bull by the horns" and sent his deputies in and "removed" supplies for distribution to the local population. This sheriff was hit with Federal charges for his actions! Someone—quick—remind me why we need the Federal government—because at this point we are not discussing theory but reality, a reality that I and tens of thousands of others lived through! This is reality—it's the reality of governmental failure, the fault of which can be placed squarely at the feet of the Federal Leviathan.

Failure: An Inherent Element of Government

When a business fails to supply consumers with quality at the best possible price in the free market that business is punished by the consumer who votes with his money and freely elects to spend his money with a competitor supplying better quality at lower price. Government operates on a different principle. While businesses must act to satisfy "we the people" as consumers, government acts to satisfy the political necessity of assuring incumbency. All decisions made by government are political decisions—yes, all decisions—even decisions made during a major disaster. Business acts economically to assure the most efficient allocation of scarce resources to satisfy consumer demand. Government, on the other hand, acts politically to protect the *status quo* or at least prevent any radical change in a two-party, liberal/conservative political system that has proven very lucrative to those in power and for those with close connections to those in power. Managers of businesses that fail lose their jobs and their reputations as effective entrepreneurs. Government bureaucrats who fail are rewarded by larger budgets! Don't believe me? What happened to the per-capita funding for Washington, D.C. schools over the past twenty years? Per-student funding has increased—indeed Washington, D.C.'s schools have one of the highest, if not the highest, per-capita funding in the country. Now take a look at the educational output—its students have one of the highest dropout rates and lowest scores on SAT exams! Another example is the increased funding voted for FEMA after its failure with Katrina! It did such a miserable job during Katrina that our politicians decided to reward the bureaucrats with more of our money! Government is a bad manager because it makes political decisions, not economic decisions. Government's decisions are always based on short time frames—present thinking—because nothing that happens after the next election is of any importance to politicians. When an apologist for government gleefully points to a successful government program as evidence of the need for government, ask him if he can prove that the free market could not have provided the same services with better quality and better price, assuming that these services were actually wanted by taxpayers in the first place. The truth is that 99% of what passes as needed government programs are actually programs that would never have been established had the consumer had the opportunity to vote. These government programs were established for political reasons to reward certain special interest groups, to enrich the political establishment, to expand government's control over society, and most importantly to assure incumbency. Vote-buying is what is happening, and even our beloved "conservative" Republicans actively engage in this short time preference political practice. When you think of Congress, Republicans and Democrats, think of a nest of grasshoppers having one hell of a good time at your expense—after all, they don't pay for the vote-buying schemes they pass, you and I do!

Government and the Origin of Katrina's Death and Destruction

Natural disasters are part of our world. We will always have them in some form or another. In a healthy free society individuals understand this and plan ahead so as to be in the best position to avoid such disasters or at least to be able to survive them. Government intervention into social planing of individuals distorts planning efforts of individuals and eventually leads to a Katrina situation in which inept political decisions result in massive death and destruction. Let's do a regression analysis of government interventions over the past seventy years or so and see what government did to create the Katrina situation.

Jefferson Parish is adjacent to Orleans Parish. Prior to Katrina the parish president had made no plans for manning the pumps during and immediately after a major hurricane. Now stop and think about this—an entire parish that is essentially below sea level, that even during a hard rainstorm must have huge pumps going to prevent flooding—massive rainfall is always associated with even minor tropical storms—and no plans (perhaps I should say no effective plans) for manning the pumps during a major hurricane? Individuals, trusting their elected officials, build and buy homes in Jefferson Parish, and then thousands of homes are flooded. Now suppose drainage and levees were the responsibility of free enterprise. Instead of having one huge monopolistic system there would be interlocking private systems so that even if one failed the entire system would not be swamped. Also, in the free market the business owners of the pumps would be personally liable for professional negligence if they fail to design and manage an efficient system and breach of contract if they fail to provide services as promised. In addition, potential homeowners could check the quality of services each provider of flood protection offered to determine if he wanted to build or purchase within the provider's service area. But because government has no market mechanism to ferret out bad providers, it just keeps on making inefficient, ineffective political decisions. For example; this same pump/drainage system in Jefferson Parish had already failed back in May of 1995! Major flooding resulted, and the political solution was simply to spend more money! Major contracts were let, and huge amounts of OPM (other people's money) were distributed to selected contractors by the politicians. One result was the dredging of the Seventeenth Street Canal. Many civil engineers have commented that perhaps this project undercut the levees and weakened them to the point that it caused or contributed to the levee collapse, resulting in the flooding of that area of New Orleans. Political decisions are never effective or efficient except as a means to redistribute OPM to friends of the powerful and assure incumbency.

Another example of government intervention leading to the Katrina situation is the Federal government's dredging of MRGO—Mississippi River Gulf Outlet (affectionately known as Mr. Go). This project was initiated by politicians who wanted to use government funds (i.e., OPM) to encourage commerce at the Port of New Orleans by giving shipping a shortcut from the Gulf of Mexico to the Port of New Orleans. The result has been to give storm surge a direct route into New Orleans! Mr. Go actually serves as a funnel to encourage storm waters to assault the levees government had previously constructed supposedly to protect New Orleans and adjacent areas. Do you notice the irony here? Government decides to build levees to protect people from storm surge, and then builds Mr. Go that serves as a conduit funneling even more storm surge into the area it built levees to protect! You can be assured that a lot of people with the "right" connections made a lot of money and exchanged many a political favor as a result of these two projects, but did "we the people" get what we "paid" for? If you look at a map of southeast Louisiana you will see that Mr. Go is southeast of New Orleans, while the Seventeenth Street Canal is northwest of New Orleans. Note how political decision-making effectively surrounded the people with imminent danger—it was just a matter of time. Even if we forgo concern about the danger introduced by Mr. Go, the economic impact originally promised as an excuse for construction of Mr. Go has been far less than expected. As a matter of fact, there are currently discussions about letting contracts (i.e., another political opportunity to spread around more OPM) to fill in Mr. Go!

So much for the recent past; let us move back to say the mid-1960s and see how government intervention back then contributed to the Katrina situation. It was the era of Lyndon Johnson's Great Society. The political decision was made that the Federal government should be massively involved in social welfare. In New Orleans massive public housing projects were initiated, food stamps and health care were provided. All of these programs encouraged people to concentrate into the small geographical areas behind Orleans Parish levees. The politicians loved it because now they had a dependable voter base that was dependent upon the political system—the politicians provided "free" housing, food, and health care, and the recipients dutifully assured incumbency at each election—what a deal! Because it was a political decision, no one dared to ask what this system of American socialism would do to the time preferences of the individuals receiving government handout. Not only did the system concentrate people behind insufficient government levees, it also actively discouraged future thinking. Generations were taught that "government will provide and protect me." They were taught not to be concerned about the future, but to live for the present because "government is here to take care of you." Government welfare removed the necessity to stay in school and learn how to become a productive member of society; it taught generations of young males that they had no responsibility for the future care and nurturing of children they fathered; it taught generations of young females that they did not need to worry about pregnancy because government would be the provider for children born out of wedlock; it taught generations that in the new world of socialized America the family was no longer necessary. Socialist welfare in contemporary America is antagonistic toward the family and the concept of individual responsibility. Civil rights became the Great Society's battle cry, but it was a new type of "rights." It was rights without responsibility. It was group rights associated with group voting to assure incumbency. Social welfare became a "right" devoid of personal responsibility and thereby contributed to the creation of a society that renounced the value of future thinking.

In the 1960s the Federal government enacted legislation creating Medicare (a form of Federal old-age socialized medical care) and encouraging states to create Medicaid (a form of socialized welfare health care). Suddenly OPM was available that encouraged the development of nursing homes—many in areas that the free market would have avoided due to the danger of massive flooding. One can only ask—"How many of those flooded nursing homes would have never been built had government not provided the massive influx of OPM?" In the early 1950s the Federal government enacted the Hill-Burton Act. This act provided large amounts of Federal monies for the "laudable" purpose of building hospitals in underserved areas—areas such as the low-lying land around New Orleans. Government intervention into the free market always produces negative repercussions—the problem is that too often the negative effects are removed in time from the interventions. Our politicians know this and have little worry that the average voter will eventually "wise up" to the politicians' destructive and cruel scheme.

In the 1930s the Federal Congress passed the Social Security Act. This act was passed for the "laudable" purpose of helping old people and preventing human want in "the sunset years of their life." The act was a spin-off of failed proposals of the American Socialist Party. Franklin Roosevelt, following the example set by German socialists under the leadership of Otto von Bismark, was successful in foisting socialism on freedom-loving Americans. One of the major repercussions of the Social Security Act was that it undercut the need for close family relations. Individuals were freed from the necessity of future thinking regarding older members of the family and were thereby encouraged to spend today and not worry about tomorrow—after all, government was there to take care of all in old age! In addition, government now began to siphon off more and more of the individual's income to finance its old-age Socialist Security program. By removing an individual worker's income in the form of taxes, government limits the individual's ability to finance future needs—thereby turning workers into vassals of America's arrogant political class.

The destructive effect of government interventions can be traced back even further: the income tax (a temporary tax in 1909 when passed!) and the inflation generator known as the Federal Reserve (1913) both act to siphon off individual income of workers causing them to become even more dependent on god-government. Working people in America are fast becoming Uncle Sam's tax slaves! Anyone who knows the history of slavery knows that a slave's time horizon is of necessity very short.

It should be evident that government, not nature, produced the perfect storm known as Katrina. As long as "we the people" keep doing what we have always done—electing "good" candidates who know how to work within the current system—then we can expect more death by government, more dependency on government, and an America where freedom, individual responsibility, and personal accountability are slowly choked to death by our democratically elected ruling elite. Changing the current system is the only real answer, but that will require people willing to engage in the arduous task of reclaiming liberty.

Addendum II

Dixie's Unwelcomed Presence in Rosie O'Donnell's America©

James Ronald Kennedy
June 21, 2008

Most Americans, including Southerners, have no problem in proclaiming that the United States is one nation indivisible. Yet, in reality there are two Americas, the Jeffersonian republic of local institutions that Southerners *imagine* they live in, and the liberal nation-state so loved by the likes of Rosie O'Donnell. Patrick Henry observed that when faced with a painful reality, "It is natural to man to indulge in the illusions of hope. We are apt to shut our eyes against a painful truth." Mr. Henry could have been describing modern evangelical Southern conservatives who refuse to recognize the fact that they live in something less than the Jeffersonian republic their founding fathers gave them.

Waging War Against America

Back in the early 1960s when the Confederate flag and things Southern were permitted to be presented on national TV in a relatively positive light, there was an episode of *The Beverly Hillbillies* in which Jethro asks Granny, "What was the Civil War?" In exasperation Granny administers a thump to Jethro's hard head and exclaims, "That was when the Yankees invaded America!" Though humorous as it was, Granny's answer contains a keen kernel of truth. From the very beginning of "America," the United States contained two divergent sections; one section, the North, was determined to use the Federal government to expropriate money and resources from the other section as a means of creating an economic empire. The other section, the South, was equally determined to protect its liberty and property while demanding simply to be "let alone." As the minority section, the South looked to the original republics of republics with its written constitution limiting the scope and power of the Federal government as a means of protecting its liberty. This was in sharp contrast to the Northern majority section that sought to use clever political stratagems to seize control of the Federal government. Once in control of the central government, it would enlarge Federal power

over the states of the minority section and then at last seize control of
the minority section and rule America in a manner that best befitted
its commercial, economic, political, and social interests. Here we
see the philosophies of the two Americas: One section believed
in the benefits of government; while the other section feared the
destructive and oppressive power of government. One section viewed
the Original Constitution as a living and socially evolving document
that should be changed at the whim of politicians and politically
appointed judges; the other section looked to the Constitution as a
contract between two diverse peoples in which those two peoples set
strict limits on the scope of power of the Federal government, while
reserving unto themselves all powers not specifically delegated to
the Federal government. The most significant reserved right held by
the minority section was the right to void the contract and establish
a new government if their reserved rights were threatened. The
marriage, i.e., union, of the numerically superior commercial North
with the numerical minority of the agricultural South, was anything
but a marriage made in heaven.

One Happy Indivisible Nation

The question of whether or not two peoples so diverse could
peacefully co-exist within one nation hung over the deliberations on
the ratification of the Constitution set before the sovereign states in
1787. Patrick Henry, Virginia's vocal anti-Federalist, tried to block the
ratification because he foresaw a time when the interests of the people
of the South would be dominated by the interests of the people of
the North. Henry saw America as two distinct and opposing peoples.
He predicted that should the South enter into a union with a people
whose commercial interests were opposed to the agricultural interests
of the South, eventually the people of the South would be dominated
by the people of the North. Most Americans would excuse this inherent
conflict by pointing to slavery and then announcing triumphantly
that the "Civil War" settled our differences—we are now one, grand,
united, and happy American family. Really—let's test this politically
correct gospel of Federal imperialism.

A recent study published by the Pew Research Center[1]

---

1. The Pew Research Center, "Trends in Political Values and Core Attitudes: 1987-
2007," www.people-press.org (accessed March 28, 2007).

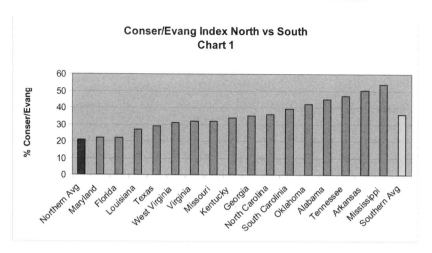

documents the continuing distinction between the America of the South and the America of the North. It must be noted that the Pew Research Center's study was not an effort to document this continuing North-South distinctiveness. The subheading for their study is "Political Landscape More Favorable to Democrats." Nevertheless, using their data we can demonstrate the fact that there are two Americas—but not the "two Americas" liberals are so fond of talking about. The Pew data demonstrates two Americas with very different *social* and political core values. For example chart number 1 is constructed from data in the Pew findings relative to the number of white evangelical, i.e., Christian, conservatives in the GOP nationwide. The Northern average (the average of all reported states less the Southern states) is 21% whereas the Southern average is 36%. Every Southern state has a larger number of "conservatives" who are self-described as white evangelicals than the Northern average. This is true even for those Southern states such as Maryland, Virginia, and Florida who have a substantial number of "non-Southern citizens."

Chart number 1 demonstrates that Southern GOP conservatives certainly have a different worldview than their Northern conservative counterparts. This difference is socially very important because that very small red bar on the left of the graph represents the Northern conservative faction in the "conservative" Republican Party that dominates the social will of "we the people" residing in every state listed to the right of that red bar! Remember Patrick Henry's warning about being in a union with people with dissimilar interests? That was then, but this is now! Same song—different verse.

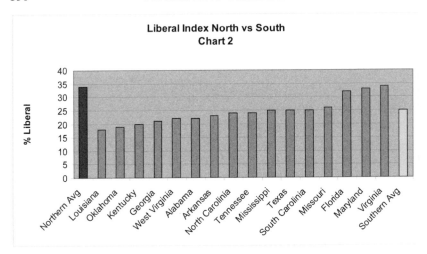

The Pew data documents that Southern conservatives in the Republican Party have a higher concern for social values than the majority of Northern conservatives in the Republican Party. Chart number 2 demonstrates that Southern Democrats are less liberal than their Northern counterparts.

The Pew research data demonstrated that approximately 34% of Northern Democrats self-described themselves as liberal. This stands in contrast to Southern Democrats where only 25% self-described themselves as liberal. Note again that, except for Virginia, every Southern state to the right of the red bar is lower than the national average. Virginia is equal to the national average. Virginia and the other two Southern states that have "enjoyed" non-Southern immigration have the highest liberal scores. Whether Southerners are in the party of Hillary Clinton or the party of George Bush, *Southern values are marginalized.* Southerners are used for the votes they bring the national (read as Northern) parties, but as a practical matter Southern core values have little influence in the elected government when those values clash with the interests of the Northern majority. The South is allowed the appearance of self-government but only so long as said self-government does not conflict with the interests of the Northern nation. The will of "we the people" of the South is dominated by those whose interests are radically different than the interests of the people of the South. Apologists for the Federal Empire will deny this, but what do the facts show?

The Façade of Representative Government

The people of the South do not have representative government; what Southerners have is a façade of representative government. To see the results of this façade all one need do is to contrast the voting pattern of the United States Congress with the votes of the elected representatives from the former thirteen Confederate States. Begin with key issues subsequent to 1965—after the passage of the Voting Rights Act of that year. What will be seen is something similar to the Pew data—the Southern representatives in Congress vote consistently more conservative than the liberal Northern majority. But the point that is imperative to understand is that Southern representatives were consistently on the *losing side* when issues that were key to the social interests of "we the people" of the South were at stake! In other words, the consent of the governed in the South has been consistently overruled and suppressed by the will of the more liberal Northern majority. Consider the sharp differences in voting patterns of Southern and non-Southern delegates in Congress: (1) 1990 act to *increase* legal immigration, non-Southern delegates voted 31% no, Southern delegates 53% no (act passed over the objections of the South); (2) 1994 assault weapons *ban*, non-Southern delegates voted 49% no, Southern delegates 66% no (the bill passed over the objections of the South), (3) 1985 bill to *restrict* the Federal court's involvement in school prayer issues, non-Southern delegates voted 63% *against* restricting the Federal courts, Southern delegates 72% *in favor* of restricting the Federal courts (liberals in favor of using Federal courts to restrict religion in schools *overrode* the will of the people of the South); (4) vote to ban forced busing[2] and (5) the recent extension of the anti-South Voting Rights Act of 1965, both passed against the will of Southern delegates to Congress.

The South finds itself in a similar condition to colonial Ireland. Although allowed votes in Parliament, the Irish were always overruled by the majority votes of the British Empire. Thus, the Irish demanded independence because they understood that the imperial majority held their interests hostage.

---

2. James R. Kennedy and Donald W. Kennedy, *Was Jefferson Davis Right?* (Gretna, LA: Pelican Publishing Company, 1998), p. 274.

Likewise, the people of the South have the appearance of democratic representation in Congress, but in reality Southern core values have never stood a chance in the Northern-dominated Federal Congress. The Southern position has been and continues to be similar to that of two Northern wolves and one Southern lamb voting on what to have for supper!

The electoral votes available to the "Civil War" Northern states and the "Civil War" Southern states is yet another measurement of the South's political captivity. A review of Tables 1 and 2 will reveal that the old Northern states are only 15 electoral votes away from naming the president in any presidential election. The South, on the other hand, is 76 votes away from electing a president. The conservative South will never be able to elect a president who truly represents *its core values*. To win a presidential election the "Civil War" North, needing only 15 more electoral votes, need only look to the states of Washington with a liberal index of 44 and holding 11 electoral votes and Colorado with a liberal index of 39 and holding 9 electoral votes. The North can win by leveraging its liberal core values.

Table 1

	"Civil War" North	Conservative Evangelical Index	Liberal Index	Electoral Vote
1	California	19	38	55
2	Connecticut	10	34	7
3	Delaware	[data not available]	[data not available]	3
4	Illinois	23	31	21
5	Indiana	33	26	11
6	Maine	25	39	4
7	Massachusetts	9	37	12
8	Michigan	25	29	17
9	Minnesota	25	35	10
11	New Hampshire	10	39	4
12	New Jersey	9	34	15
13	New York	10	35	31
14	Ohio	24	29	20
15	Oregon	26	44	7
16	Pennsylvania	23	28	21
17	Rhode Island	[data not available]	32	4

18	Vermont	[data not available]	[data not available]	3
19	Wisconsin	21	31	10
	Average/ Total	**20**	**34**	**255**

Table 2

	"Civil War" South	**Conservative Evangelical Index**	**Liberal Index**	**Electoral Vote**
1	Alabama	45	22	9
2	Arkansas	50	23	6
3	Florida	22	32	27
4	Georgia	35	21	15
5	Kentucky	34	20	8
6	Louisiana	27	18	9
7	Maryland	22	33	10
8	Mississippi	54	25	6
9	Missouri	32	26	11
10	North Carolina	36	24	15
11	Oklahoma	42	19	7
12	South Carolina	39	25	8
13	Tennessee	47	24	11
14	Texas	29	25	34
15	Virginia	32	34	13
16	West Virginia	31	22	5
	Average/ Total	**36**	**25**	**194**

[270 Electoral Votes Needed to Win Presidency]

The only way the South can "win" is to forego allegiance to its core values and support a national Republican carpetbagger candidate such as George W. Bush. The national Republican Party holds the South hostage—Southerners either accept the GOP's favorite neo-conservative, or else she can look forward to being ruled by scalawag presidents such as Lyndon Baines Johnson and Bill Clinton!

Rosie O'Donnell's America

The existence of two Americas, one Northern and one Southern, was also demonstrated in a recent study of charitable giving in America. This study documents that Southerners give much more to charitable causes than do their Northern counterparts. Indeed the people of Mississippi, the poorest state in the Federal Empire, give more to charity than the people of the rich state of Massachusetts! Remember that Mississippi's evangelical/conservative index was reported as 54% and her liberal index was reported as 25%, whereas Massachusetts' index was 9% (Evang/Con) and 37% (Liberal). Here we see stark evidence of the influence that core values have on the social actions of two very different people. Yet the people of Massachusetts (the Barney Franks and Teddy Kennedys) in league with their ideological fellows in other Northern states dominate the political will of the people of Mississippi and her sister states of the South. To most "Americans" it is not unusual to have a political system where the majority in the North force their will upon the minority in the South—"it's the way things have always been." The publication of the results of the charitable giving study caused no small amount of consternation among Northern liberals. After all, the liberal establishment's press and Hollywood are constantly reminding America, "Liberals care more for people than conservatives." But now the irony; along comes a study documenting that Southerners living in the poorest part of America, the very seat of traditional American Christianity and conservatism, are voluntarily giving far in excess to that of the people living in the virtuous and prosperous North. In their relative poverty Southerners are out-giving prosperous liberal Northerners. Such facts had to be "explained" and who better to explain than the one contemporary American who typifies Northern liberalism—Rosie O'Donnell.

Shortly after the charitable giving results were released and picked up by numerous news sources it became a topic of discussion on the daytime television program *The View*. Rosie quickly dismissed the thought that perhaps Northern liberals were not as caring as they claim by declaring that of course liberals do not give to charities because liberals work to make sure government provides for the needy! Rosie's America is a place where big government forces huge tax levies upon productive people to pay for government programs for special interest groups. Rosie's America is one in which private property is held at the tax collector's discretion. Rosie's America is a place in which America's politicians, the majority of whom are elected by the Northern liberal majority, decide how best to redistribute people's income. Rosie's America is a place where public dependency has replaced individual responsibility. Rosie's America is a place where nanny government has replaced family responsibility. Rosie's America is a place where faith in god-government has replaced faith in the living God. Rosie's America is the opposite of Thomas Jefferson's America, a place where government would rest so lightly upon its citizens that they would hardly feel its presence. Again the distinction between the two Americas, the liberal North and the Christian conservative South, is about the differing core values and attitudes toward the role of government in society. Southerners would prefer to live in Thomas Jefferson's America, but the liberal national majority forces the South to accept its assigned place in Rosie's America.

But Does All of This Really Make Any Difference?

Some would argue that traditional Southern conservatives—those who adhere to the political philosophy espoused by Southerners such as John C. Calhoun, Jefferson Davis, Patrick Henry, and Thomas Jefferson—are out of touch with reality. "That was then, this is now," they caustically proclaim as they consign traditional Southern conservative values to the trash bin of history. "Current reality," they patronizingly assert, "requires us to work with today's American political system—and anyway, people are no longer interested in such arcane Jeffersonian arguments." They argue that Southerners are no longer interested in constitutional government, limiting the scope of Federal intrusion into our society, or defending their personal liberty. The assumption they promote is that the South is no different than the rest of America. In general, they assert, the people of the South have the same desires, opinions, hopes, and fears as the rest of America. Of course they must maintain this position because it is the only way they can justify Northern liberal majority rule imposed upon the Southern people.

For the sake of discussion let us assume they are right. Let us assume that the Southern people are just as dumbed-down as other Americans; assume that the social rot and corruption that is typified by Hollywood is equally shared by Southerners; assume that the people of the South are just as concerned about advancing the civil rights of homosexuals as the people in Rosie's America; assume that Southerners have renounced their proud traditions of limited Federalism, State's Rights, local self-government, and personal responsibility before a living God—assume all of this and then see if the people of the South are "better off" as a result of abandoning the faith of their Colonial and Confederate Fathers.

In the materialistic world of Rosie's America money is still the bottom line. Rosie, as with all socialists and liberals, avoids giving her money to charities because she wants to use the police power of government's tax collector to expropriate other people's money to use for those social causes that liberal political elites determine as worthy of your money. The impact of taxes and inflation (a hidden tax)[3] are negligible for those with high income and close connections with those who hold the power of government. People who must live on relatively smaller incomes and who have no close connections with the powers-that-be in government bear a disproportionately larger share of the cost of government. In Rosie's America "we the people of the South" have a much lower per capita income than the people in the rest of the country. Liberals have used slavery and segregation as an explanation as to why so many Southerners have a lower personal income when compared to the rest of America. One would think that the economic expansion enjoyed by the nation in the 142 years since the close of the "War" would have eliminated the presumed economic disadvantage of slavery. Add to that the money government has spent fighting poverty since the removal of government-enforced segregation laws—estimates run from 600 billion up to 7 trillion dollars[4]—and one would certainly think that the funding of liberal/socialist social engineering projects would have removed the taint of poverty from the South. So the question is again asked: "Are the people of the South better off in Rosie's America—better off than they would be if they were living in Thomas Jefferson's America?" Chart number 3 answers this most important question with a resounding NO!

No, the people of the South are not better off as a result of being obedient subjects in Rosie's America. The per capita income for the USA is $30,472.00, whereas the Southern per capita income

3. James Ronald Kennedy, *Reclaiming Liberty* (Gretna, LA: Pelican Publishing Company, 2005), pp. 127-45.

4. Ibid., pp. 134 & 106.

Per Captia Income Southern States Compairson

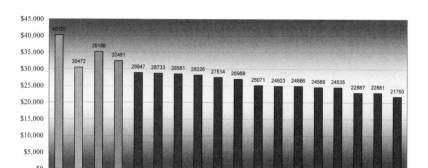

is $26,260.00—16% less! With the exception of Maryland and Virginia, every Southern state is below the national per capita income. The reason for the higher levels of income for Virginia and Maryland is explained by looking at the per capita income for those residing in the nation's capital—it pays to have close political connections with those who control the empire's perks and privileges! Virginia and Maryland have large numbers of these government functionaries residing within their borders, thereby artificially raising their per capita income. Even if we assume the people of the South have sold or rejected their inheritance of Jeffersonian liberty for the promise of being part of the prosperous nation—we are still left with the cruel fact that our "fellow" Americans have not delivered on their promise. Once again the data demonstrates two Americas—the prosperous liberal Northern nation, and the impoverished South.

The Insidious Consequences of Self-Delusion

Why do the people of the South continue to tolerate and support the political system that systematically oppresses their core values and liberty? The Northern liberal majority can afford to tolerate their peculiar subjects in Dixie, but can the people of Dixie afford to continue accepting political domination? Southerners can continue to delude themselves by asserting that they are part of "one nation, indivisible, with liberty and justice for all"—and with passionate patriotism break into yet another stanza of the "Battle Hymn of the

Republic." Patriotism to a nation-state that rejects core Southern values is the opium used by politicians and neo-conservative talking heads to allay Southern discontent. To maintain a pacified South, the national majority must continually labor to repress the truth that a republic based on liberty is not indivisible. Jeffersonian republicans understand that only empires are indivisible, and all too often empires are held together at the point of a bloody bayonet. Regardless of how often pacified Southerners hold their hands over their hearts and pledge fidelity to a nation that promises "justice for all," it will not change the fact that Southerners will never receive justice in the present Northern liberal-dominated political system. *Self-delusion is the prerequisite to self-destruction.* With each passing election the South becomes less like the traditional Christian conservative South and more like the liberal Northern nation. Each year Dixie devolves into an impoverished Southern version of Rosie's America. How long will the people of the South continue to cooperate with those who hate the very core values by which Southerners define their society?

There are two Americas in the United States today: Rosie's America of the Northern liberal majority that can afford to wait for the slow demise of the other America; and the other America of traditional Jeffersonian conservatives that with each passing generation forgets or foregoes its inheritance of Christianity and of liberty. The second America cannot afford an indefinite wait—*a radical change must take place in the thinking of the Southern people if they are to survive and pass their inheritance of constitutional liberty and Christianity to the next generation.* The opium of blind, unthinking, memorized patriotism must be rejected and replaced with allegiance to the principle of liberty. Patrick Henry's observation must become the South's reason for being: "The first thing I have at heart is American *liberty*; the second thing is American *Union*," or as John C. Calhoun declared: "The Union, next to our liberties—most dear."

Evidence abounds demonstrating that there are two Americas. Recently ESPN conducted a poll asking whether the people of South Carolina should be allowed to fly the Confederate flag on their state capitol grounds. Voters from Southern states voted overwhelmingly in favor of flying the Confederate flag, while voters from Northern states voted against flying the Confederate flag in South Carolina. Another poll conducted by *Fox News* regarding gun rights demonstrated 62% of Southerners are gun owners, whereas only 27% of Northeasterners own guns. Yet, the Northern majority has the power to encroach at will upon the Second Amendment rights of Southerners—majority rule! The people of the South must accept their position as a dominated minority in Rosie's America or be willing to make a radical change in their efforts of defending Southern core values.

The radical change needed will not come from business-as-usual conservatives. Every conservative politician has a vested interest in preserving the *status quo*—they can be expected to fight against radical change more so than their liberal counterparts. If radical change is to come, it will come from a true outsider—someone who has no vested interest in maintaining the *status quo,* someone interested in replacing the current political model with one based on liberty! It is not a matter of can it be done—it is a matter of should it be done. It is often said that "silence gives consent." Will the people of the South continue to silently consent to having their values dominated by the numerical majority of Rosie's America? Will they continue their insidious acts of self-delusion? Or will they rise up and declare that they will no longer be "unequally yoked together with unbelievers."[5] *Deo Vindice.*

5. 2 Corinthians 6:14.

Addendum III

Consent of the Governed— Key to Liberty[1]
Walter Donald Kennedy

"Governments are instituted among men, deriving their just Powers from the Consent of the governed..."

Declaration of Independence

The unanimous declaration of the delegates of the thirteen United States in 1776 announced to the world the great American principle that free people have a right and a duty to give their consent to any form of government that exists over them. More to the point, a free people have the obligation to change any form of government radically which has proven itself to be destructive to their "Unalienable Rights."

Thomas Jefferson, in writing the Declaration of Independence, drew deeply from the writings of John Locke. Indeed, a reading of Locke's *Two Treatises of Government* will clearly demonstrate the relationship between it and Jefferson's ideas of "government by consent" and the obligation of a people to replace a tyrannical government with one that rules by the consent of the governed. Although Jefferson borrowed from Locke, it should be noted that Locke's theories of consent and the right of a free people to replace a tyrannical government are restatements of Rev. Samuel Rutherford's theories as taught in his book, *Lex Rex*.

These two principles of government, so nobly enunciated by the founding fathers of this republic, have many worthy antecedents. Nevertheless, it was by the hands and efforts of the Patriots of 1776 that these two "Keys to Liberty" were boldly placed upon the political stage.

---

1. This piece was originally published in James Ronald Kennedy and Walter Donald Kennedy, *Why Not Freedom!* (Gretna, LA: Pelican Publishing Company, 1994).

Locke points out that an institution of government is given power by a "community" of people for the exclusive reason of "...the Mutual Preservation of their Lives, Liberty, and Estates... Property." Locke notes that when these ends of government are no longer being met, the "community" retains the right to recall that trust given to government: "[When trust] is Manifestly neglected... the trust must necessarily be forfeited." Here, Locke is describing the ultimate secession movement. When faced with a government that has overstepped its legitimately entrusted power, people of a sovereign community have a duty to withdraw from that threatening institution. Liberty, not governmental institutions, is foremost in Locke's theory of government, regardless of the type of institution, be it a king, a president, a congress, or a *union*! During the great debate which culminated in the adoption of the United States Constitution and Bill of Rights, Patrick Henry echoed the same sentiments. Henry, while advocating American Union, nevertheless, made it clear where his first loyalty would remain when he stated, "The first thing I have at heart is American *liberty*; the second thing is American Union." Not only did Patrick Henry, a leading anti-Federalist, address the question of the relationship of a community and its government, but also a leading Federalist defended the right of a people to abolish any form of government that no longer served their needs. James Madison, in *Federalist Papers No. 43*, states "...the safety and happiness of society are the objects at which all political institutions must be sacrificed." Madison makes it clear that the safety and happiness of society are to take precedence over any institution of government or even government itself.

Why does Locke, when considering the protection of man's freedom, place such emphasis upon the withdrawal of a people's consent to a government? The right of a people to withdraw from a threatening government, i.e., to secede, is a simple act of self-protection and of self-preservation of unalienable rights. The individual rights of the people of a community to be secure in their right of life, liberty, and property, along with their collective right as a "community" (consent of the governed) will always take precedence over governmental institutions. As Locke declared, "Men can never be secure from Tyranny, if there be no means to escape it." Secession is the means by which a sovereign community escapes from tyranny.

Now let us reread Jefferson's famous Declaration where he states, "That whenever any form of government becomes destructive of these ends [life, liberty, and pursuit of happiness], it is the right of the people to alter or to abolish it." When the king's government refused to recognize the rights of British subjects in America, the people of each colonial "community," in an act of self-defense and self-protection, seceded from the British Union. They did so only for the protection of their unalienable rights.

Now let us look at Jefferson Davis' Inaugural Address: "The right solemnly proclaimed at the birth of the United States...undeniably recognizes in the people the power to resume the authority delegated for the purposes of government." Note that in both 1776 and 1861 secession is viewed as a means of protecting liberty. Locke's theory of "consent" proved to be the foundation of two American secession movements and, no doubt, will always serve as a foundation for those who reject the tyrannical notion of an all-powerful government.

Addendum IV

Boom-Bust Economics
James Ronald Kennedy

"My 401k has turned into a 201k!"

The Forgotten Man's Lament

Have you ever noticed that whenever there is some type of "economic" crisis Democratic and Republican politicians, who as a ruling elite have run American government since 1861, always force the taxpayer to fund the political "solution" to a problem "we the people" did not create?

Booms, Busts, Bubbles—What Are They, and What Did We Do to Deserve Them?

"We the people" did not create the infamous Dot-Com Bubble (1995-2001) in which more than $5 trillion of stock value and major investments were wiped out. "We the people" did not create the current housing bubble (2001-2009), but rest assured we will be the ones who eventually pay for other people's unsound economic decisions. Economic bubbles are not new, but today they are coming much closer together, and the losses they generate are spread across almost the entire economy. In 1717 John Law used his connections with the French monarchy to start a land deal in North America that went from boom to bust in a matter of three years—it was known as the Mississippi Bubble. John Law could not have perpetrated his scheme without the assistance of the French ruling elite. In this way the Mississippi Bubble is similar to our current economic bubbles, but unlike our current bubbles the economic impact of the bursting of the Mississippi Bubble was felt only by those relatively few individuals who had invested in John Law's New World venture. Government, in our modern world, uses its taxing and regulatory schemes to encourage working men and women to invest in the stock market via systems such as 401k retirement funds. When bubbles burst today, virtually all productive, hard-working, thrifty Americans suffer a negative impact in their retirement portfolio. Are these losses the result of normal market risks that are a natural part of free-market investments, or are other forces at work—forces basically unknown and outside of the control of the average person?

A boom-bust cycle is not a normal aspect of the free market. Some may confuse it with the normal business cycle that naturally occurs to one degree or another in all businesses. Business cycles are a result of the free-market balancing of supply with demand. When demand is increased, it takes time for businesses to increase production to supply the volume demanded by consumers. Because equilibrium between supply and demand is never actually achieved (forget about all those dull classes explaining supply-demand curves with a specific point of intersection called the market clearance point that most college students sleep through in Economics 101) there is always movement above or below the point where supply equals demand. This is caused by the time delay between consumers sending their demand message, and businesses gearing up to meet the new level of demand. The business cycle reverses when supply exceeds demand and businesses must reduce output. Business cycles are a normal aspect of the free market. The boom-bust cycle on the other hand is caused by government interfering with the free market via its regulatory, law-making, and taxing policies. In the free market, productive entrepreneurs will seek new or more efficient methods to supply goods and services demanded by consumers. Productive entrepreneurs in the free market allocate limited capital (investment dollars) to those activities that consumers (society) value the highest. When government interferes in the market place with its taxing policy, regulations, or laws, it distorts the market's ability to efficiently allocate scarce resources and causes inefficient and therefore unsustainable use of these scarce resources. Government actions are misleading and actually draw investments away from sound business opportunities and cause a net decrease in the vitality of the sustainable economy. The government's tax policy, laws, and regulations support and encourage parasitic entrepreneurs while it hinders, limits, and confuses the activities of productive entrepreneurs.

Any successful farmer or small business person knows that if you are using your resources inefficiently then you may not make a profit or at a minimum you will not make as much as your more efficient competitors. When government causes an inefficient allocation of scarce investment resources, the entire economy suffers an opportunity loss—jobs, profits, and investment income that could have been generated never happen. This opportunity loss represents prosperity foregone, but because it is not seen by the public it is a loss we all suffer, but it is an invisible loss. We are not as economically well off as we should be, but we just don't know why. This of course works to the tremendous advantage of the ruling elite—invisible losses caused by politicians are safe losses because no one can prove that politicians caused the nonappearance of new jobs, profits, or investment income. The important thing for working men and women to remember is that inefficient and unsustainable investments will eventually be exposed by the market, and when they are eventually exposed, their temporary boom will quickly become a bust, creating losses that must be paid—and guess who gets to pay—you guessed it—you and I and all other taxpayers must pony up the necessary revenue to fund the bailout or otherwise pay for the losses "we the people" did not create.

Modern economic booms occur when the government's central bank injects new money into the economy. The Federal Reserve (Fed) serves the role of a central bank in the United States. This new money is not based on increased productivity or an increase of a commodity, usually gold and silver, held by the Fed, but it is money created out of thin air. Austrian economists refer to it as fiat money—government paper claiming value where none actually exists! Generally the Fed does not rely on the printing of new money. Most of the money the Fed pumps into the economy is created by issuing loans or credit to its member banks. In the free market, loans can only be made as a result of accumulated savings. But the Fed treats credit the same as it would fiat money and creates it out of thin air—it issues loans to its member banks that are not backed by savings on hand. This new money or credit entering the economy creates the boom phase in which entrepreneurs seek to make profits by investing in what appears to be promising (profitable and sustainable) enterprises—but because of all of the heated economic activity going on during the boom it is impossible to tell which investments are, in fact, sustainable. Of course when the bust comes it is easy to know which investments are unsound, but by then it is too late for the average investor.

Did You and I Create the Housing Bubble?

In 2008 America's politicians were forced to admit that the economy had experienced a housing bubble and now—oh my God, can you believe it—the economy was experiencing the inevitable bust that follows all bubbles. An economic bubble arises during the boom phase of all "free-market" economies that are hampered by a governmental central bank. The central bank attempts to stimulate the economy by injecting money (liquidity) into the economy. This new money is created out of thin air—it has nothing to back it up, and therefore has no actual value, but those who get first use of this new money get to use it at face value. As the new money moves through the economy it dilutes the value of existing money, and by the time the last person in the economic feeding chain gets the money its true value is equal to the diluted value of all money in use in the economy.[1] The new money, created out of thin air, injected into the economy by the central bank has the same effect as the fleet coming to home port and thousands of sailors coming ashore with money in hand—a tremendous but temporary boost to the economy. The distinct difference is the sailors earned their money, and they are holding old money that does not further dilute the value of the currency then in circulation. The central bank's money is not "earned"; that is, it has nothing of real value to back it up—no increase in productivity or a commodity such as a precious metal that justifies the existence of the new money. This new money is a political fiction—a cruel fiction that serves the purpose of those who first use it but is devalued by the time the last holder gets the use of the new money—and you know who the last holder will be—the forgotten man—the only innocent party in the whole affair.

---

1. The author acknowledges that this explanation is a very simple description of a complicated economic issue. To those desiring a detailed study I recommend *What Has Government Done to Our Money?* by Murray Rothbard as a beginning and a visit to the leading Austrian (true free market) Web site: www.mises.org.

The Federal Reserve (Fed) uses its ability to control the interest rate it charges large financial institutions for loans to stimulate the economy. In the lead up to the bust of the housing bubble the Fed lowered its interest rate to 0 to 0.25%—the lowest ever![2] The Fed was trying to keep the economic boom going and spare the ruling elite the political pain that always arises when a boom turns into a bust. The central bank in Japan during the 1990s lowered their interest rate to zero in an attempt to keep their boom going—it did not work, and their economy experienced a decade of slow and painful recovery. Recovery from the Fed-induced boom-bust cycle is always painful, but when politicians try to prevent the pain all they do is increase both the length and depth of the pain. A better idea is for "we the people" to establish a free-market system in which the parasitic ruling class cannot create the boom-bust cycle in the first place.

If this is correct, you may ask, then why do we allow "our" politicians to use America's central bank so recklessly? The answer is that there is a lot of "smoke and mirrors" and special interests associated with politicians, central banks, unsupported money (fiat money), the Fed's interest rate adjustments, and the Fed's issuing of credit out of thin air to large Wall Street financial institutions. For one thing, there is always a time lag between issuing fiat money, credit not supported by savings, adjustments to the Fed's interest rate, and the eventual downside of such artificial "tinkering" with the free market. This time lag between the initial boom, the development of an economic bubble, and the eventual economic bust gives politicians and Fed chairmen "creditable deniability" when the economic disaster ultimately becomes apparent. It is an extremely effective political use of the old technique of the pickpocket crying "stop thief," while pointing to an innocent person, and then in the ensuing confusion the thief escapes. For example; we all have seen and heard Representative Barney Frank, Senator Chris Dobb, and President Barack Obama lamenting the greed of unscrupulous business people during

---

2. Thomas E. Woods, *Meltdown: A Free-Market Look at Why the Stock Market Collapsed, the Economy Tanked, and Government Bailouts Will Make Things Worse* (Washington, DC: Regnery Publishing, Inc., 2009), p. 77.

the discussion (you cannot call it a debate) about the 2008-2009 bailout of Wall Street financial institutions. The truth is that these artificial business "opportunities" would never have occurred in a true free-market economy but for the political interventions of parasitic politicians such as Frank, Dodd, and Obama!

Business people in a true free market (productive entrepreneurs) look to invest in sustainable and reliable business opportunities, and it punishes, with economic loss and/or bankruptcy, those business people who make unsound investment decisions. But thanks to politicians like Frank, Dodd, and Obama, a system of laws have been passed that (1) mandated—as in affirmative action— loans to people who would never have been given credit in a true free market; (2) established a central bank that could provide money and credit out of thin air; and (3) provided actual and implied guarantees that loans made to those who would never have qualified in a true free market would be insured against default by American taxpayers. For their own political advantage America's ruling elite have perverted the free-market system from one that encourages productive entrepreneurs to one that enables parasitic entrepreneurial activities. These parasitic entrepreneurial activities are initially very rewarding—profit-generating—but eventually the free market reveals such artificial, nonproductive investments to be unsustainable, and the economic bust begins. When these unsound investments are shown to be unsustainable it becomes evident that someone has to pay for the loss—the question is who will pay?

As all working people know "there is no such thing as a free lunch." Someone will eventually have to pay for these parasitic and unsound investments. Usually the stock market takes a major hit as prices plummet. Those innocent productive people who invested their real savings, such as retirement funds, in the stock market find out that their 401k now has a significantly smaller value as the "market adjustment" takes place. "Market adjustment" is a euphemism for making the productive element of society pay for the unsound investments of the parasitic element of society. Notice how politicians and those close to the ruling elite—the Federal Reserve, big banking houses, and Wall Street financial institutions—all earn a substantial profit or garner other benefits from the economic boom, but "we the people" end up financing the "market adjustments" necessary to liquidate the unsound investments made during the government-inspired boom period. The innocent (productive) parties pay, while the guilty (parasitic) parties escape to begin yet another boom-bust cycle. While you and I did not create the housing bubble, under America's current political system, you and I are forced to pay for it!

Republican or Democrat—It Makes No Difference

America's ruling elite is composed of both Republicans and Democrats. In reality the two-party system is nothing more than an exclusive club in which friendly but competitive rivals compete to see which one has their turn controlling the reins of Federal power. The primary purpose of both parties is to maintain the *status quo*—keep the parasitic political system operating in a business-as-usual mode. America's ruling elite operate in a manner similar to the Royal Court in a medieval monarchy. Those who were a part of the monarchy or who had close connections with the Royal Court reaped the benefits of power. Those who had no such connections were the ones who were forced to pay the taxes to fund the monarchy. A major difference was that the king planned to be around for a long time and thus had a long time horizon when devising tax policies, rules, and regulations that would impact the productivity of his subjects. The king wanted his subjects to be productive in order to pay more taxes in the future. Politicians, on the other hand, who control power in America, have a short time horizon of two to six years. Politicians want to gain the most they can in the shortest time possible because they know they will face the possibility of being replaced in the next election. Their motive is to "get as much as we can now because if we leave anything it may be used next year by our opponents."

Both parties spend an inordinate amount of time blaming the other party for whatever crises may be in vogue at the time. The truth is that they both are equally guilty. But to gain power (or maintain office once elected) they must convince "we the people" that the other party is at fault. On election day "we the people" then get to decide which party is at fault when in reality both parties are at fault and regardless of which one wins the election the *status quo* will remain secure and intact. As long as the current parasitic political system remains intact, the boom-bust economic cycles will continue; the ruling elite and those close to the ruling elite will do well during these cycles because "we the people" will pay the final bill. How did we get ourselves into such a sad situation?

In 1913 politicians alone with their friends and supporters in large banking institutions on Wall Street promised Americans that if Congress would establish a central bank—or at least a Federal Reserve—then they would be able to control the boom-bust economic cycles. Americans were assured that if they would allow the ruling elite to create the Fed, then "we the people" would be spared the rigors of the boom-bust cycles. Like all political promises, the promise that the Fed could control boom-bust cycles was soon forgotten. Between 1913 and 1990 America suffered through approximately sixteen recessions or depressions (depending on how they defined the depression and recession). This is not exactly a good track record, but for some reason the ruling elite has never expressed a desire to undo the Fed and allow the free market to establish interest rates and our money supply. Obviously someone with great power is gaining as a result of the *status quo.*

In the late 1970s President Richard Nixon, a "conservative" Republican, took America off the gold standard (or at least what was left of the gold standard) and announced with great glee that "we are all Keynesians now." John Maynard Keynes (1883-1946) was the architect of modern nominal socialism. He was a British economist whose economic theory requires government to manage the economy by massive government projects and the infusion of government-created money—the ruling elite now call it deficit financing—you and I would call it spending money you really don't have.

John Maynard Keynes viewed the free-market capitalist system as a failure and wanted to replace it with a quasi-free market in which the government would use regulations, government projects, and government money to manage the economy. But as we have witnessed, such government interventions into the free market pervert the market and redirect entrepreneurs from productive activity to parasitic activity. Capital (money) that would have been used by productive entrepreneurs to create real and sustainable economic activity is diverted by government intervention into nonproductive, unsustainable (parasitic) activities that will eventually be paid for by the taxpayer. Yet, even though we have years full of examples of the Fed's failure, there has never been a Republican president or presidential nominee who was willing to renounce Richard Nixon's infamous quote—the truth is that with perhaps one exception all national Republicans in Washington, D. C. are still Keynesians. The Republican Party is just as wedded to the *status quo* as the Democratic Party. Each party has its own set of special interest groups that receive favored treatment when their party controls power, but both parties can be counted on to do whatever it takes to maintain the ruling elite's control and parasitic use of Federal power.

"We the people" who obey the law, pay the taxes, and maintain traditional Christian moral values have become America's forgotten people—the proverbial forgotten man. The forgotten man has had many laments to describe this sad state of affairs—"My take-home pay won't take me home!"; "The rich get richer while the poor get poorer"—but now he has a new one—"My 401k has become a 201k!" The sad reality is that in all of these laments the forgotten man is complaining against a reality in which he is buffeted about by mysterious forces seemingly beyond his control, and when taking into account all the actors in this tragedy—he alone is the only innocent party, and he alone has no one to protect his interests.

Bibliography

Books

Bork, Robert. *Slouching Towards Gomorrah: Modern Liberalism and American Decline.* New York: Regan Books, 1996.

Bradford, M. E. *Founding Fathers: Brief Lives of the Framers of the United States Constitution.* Lawrence, KS: The University Press of Kansas, 1981.

————*Original Intentions: On the Making and Ratification of the United States Constitution.* Athens, GA: The University Press of Georgia, 1993.

Calhoun, John C. "A Disquisition on Government." *The Works of John C. Calhoun, Vol. I.* New York, D. Appleton and Company, MDCCLIV.

Dalrymple, Theodore. *Our Culture, What's Left of It.* Chicago: Ivan R. Dee, 2005.

Griffin, Edward G. *The Fearful Master.* Boston: Western Islands Publishers, 1964.

Kennedy, James Ronald. *Reclaiming Liberty.* Gretna, LA: Pelican Publishing Company, 2005.

Kennedy, James Ronald and Walter Donald Kennedy. *The South Was Right!* Gretna, LA: Pelican Publishing Company, 1994.

————*Why Not Freedom!* Gretna, LA: Pelican Publishing Company, 1995.

Kennedy, James R. and Walter D. Kennedy. *Was Jefferson Davis Right?* Gretna, LA: Pelican Publishing Company, 1998.

Kennedy, Walter Donald and Al Benson, Jr. *Red Republicans and Lincoln's Marxists: Marxism in the Civil War.* Bloomington, IN: iUniverse, 2007 .

Llosa, Alvaro Vargas, "The Case of Latin America." *Making Poor Nations Rich,* Benjamin Powell, ed. Stanford, CA: Stanford University Press, 2008.

Lukacs, John. *Democracy and Populism: Fear and Hatred.* New Haven and London: Yale University Press, 2005.

Mencken, H. L. *Prejudices,* 2nd Series. New York: Knopf, 1924.

Moore and Lake. *The American's Guide to the Constitution of the United States of America.* Trenton, NJ: 1813.

Mother Teresa. *Jesus Is My All in All.* Brian Kolodiejchuk, M. C. ed. New York: Doubleday, 2008.

Parker, Star. *Uncle Sam's Plantation.* Nashville, TN: WND Books, 2003.

Quirk, William J. and R. Randall Birdwell. *Judicial Dictatorship.* New Brunswich, NJ: Transaction Publishers, 1995.

Rothbard, Murray. *What Has Government Done to Our Money?* Auburn, AL: Ludwig von Mises Institute, 1991.

Von Mises, Ludwig. *Human Action: A Treatise on Economics.* 1949, Auburn, AL: Ludwig von Mises Institute, 1998.

Woods, Thomas E. Jr. *The Church and The Market: A Catholic Defense of the Free Market.* New York: Lexington Books, 2005.

————*Meltdown: A Free-Market Look at Why the Stock Market Collapsed, the Economy Tanked, and Government Bailouts Will Make Things Worse.* Washington, DC: Regnery Publishing, Inc., 2009.

Court Cases

Barron v. Baltimore, 7 Peters 243 (1833).

Online Sources

Patrick J. Buchanan, "Systemic Failure," http://www.humanevents.com/article.php?id=31154, accessed March 20, 2009.

The Pew Research Center, "Trends in Political Values and Core Attitudes: 1987-2007," www.people-press.org, accessed March 28, 2007.

Williams, Walter E., "A Nation of Cowards," February 25, 2009, www.townhall.com, accessed February 26, 2009.

www.dailymail.co.uk/news/worldnews/article-1169030/Pope-warns-desert-godlessness-Good-Friday-address.html, accessed April 12, 2009.

www.gallup.com/poll/114022/State-States-Importance-Religiion.aspx?version=print, accessed March 21, 2009.

www.pbs.org/fmc/interviews/moynihan.htm, accessed April 12, 2009.

www.vaughns-1-pagers.com/politics/red-blue-states-summary.htm, accessed March 21, 2009.

Periodicals

Lerrick, Adam, "Obama and the Tax-Tipping Point," *The Wall Street Journal,* Wednesday, October 22, 2008.

The Federalist Papers, No. 28, No. 32, and No. 85.

The Free Market, Vol. 27, No. 1, January 2009.

Index